Chile

Chile

BY MICHAEL BURGAN

Enchantment of the World™
Second Series

CHILDREN'S PRESS®

An Imprint of Scholastic Inc.

Frontispiece: **Hot springs in Panguipulli**

Consultant: Morris Rossabi, PhD, Senior Scholar and Adjunct Professor, Department of East Asian Languages and Cultures, Columbia University, New York, New York

Please note: All statistics are as up-to-date as possible at the time of publication.

Book production by The Design Lab

Library of Congress Cataloging-in-Publication Data
Names: Burgan, Michael, author.
Title: Chile / by Michael Burgan.
Description: New York : Children's Press, an imprint of Scholastic Inc.,
   [2016] | Series: Enchantment of the world | Includes bibliographical
   references and index.
Identifiers: LCCN 2015048543 | ISBN 9780531218853 (library binding)
Subjects: LCSH: Chile—Juvenile literature.
Classification: LCC F3058.5 .B87 2016 | DDC 983—dc23 LC record available at http://lccn
.loc.gov/2015048543

1 2 3 4 5 6 7 8 9 10 R 26 25 24 23 22 21 20 19 18 17

Mural in Valparaíso

Contents

CHAPTER 1   Welcome to Chile! 8

CHAPTER 2   A Land of Extremes 12

CHAPTER 3   In the Wild 26

CHAPTER 4   Creating Chile 38

CHAPTER 5   A Strong Democracy 60

CHAPTER 6   A Growing Economy **70**

CHAPTER 7   The People of Chile **80**

CHAPTER 8   Spiritual Life **90**

CHAPTER 9   Arts and Entertainment **100**

CHAPTER 10   Living and Playing **112**

Timeline **128**

Fast Facts **130**

To Find Out More **134**

Index **136**

Left to right: **Torres del Paine National Park, Valparaíso, guanacos, fishing, Cuasimodo festival**

CHAPTER 1

Welcome to Chile!

8

STROLL THROUGH THE STREETS OF SANTIAGO, THE capital of Chile, and you'll see the hustle and bustle of a major city. More than five million people call Santiago home, and it's a center for arts and business. The city sits almost in the middle of Chile, a long, thin country wedged between the Pacific Ocean and the Andes, the longest and highest mountain range in South America.

The sea and the mountains help define Chile. The Pacific provides food and a way to ship goods all over the world. The spectacular snow-covered peaks of the Andes attract tourists to Chile and shape its weather. In some areas, the tall mountains help draw moisture from the air, providing much-needed rain.

That moisture is rare in Chile's north, which is dominated by the Atacama Desert, one of the driest places on earth. Far to the south is a region called Patagonia, which Chile shares with neighboring Argentina. Patagonia has been called Chile's frontier. The landscape is rugged and people often travel by ferry in areas where no roads exist.

Opposite: **The Andes Mountains tower above the gleaming skyscrapers of Santiago, Chile's capital.**

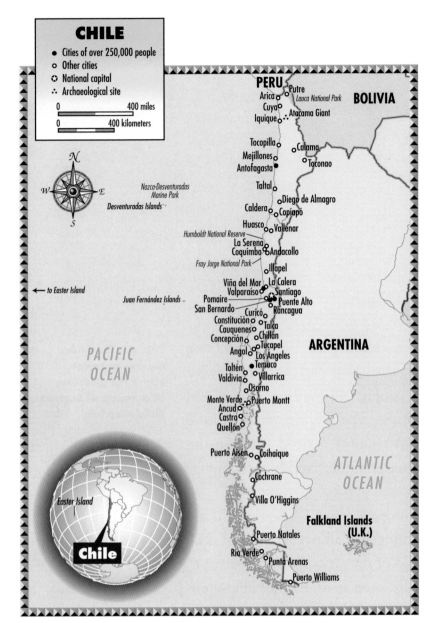

Patagonia and the rest of Chile were once the home of several different indigenous, or native, peoples. Today, the Mapuche are the largest indigenous group in Chile. Over the centuries, many were forced off their lands and moved to cities to find jobs. Today, some are trying to reclaim the land they lost.

The Mapuche have seen waves of settlers come to their lands and the rest of Chile. The Spanish came first and had the largest impact. Parts of Chile were a Spanish colony for more than 250 years beginning in the 1540s. Today, Spanish is Chile's national language, and Roman Catholicism—Spain's major religion—is Chile's major faith.

In later years, immigrants from other parts of Europe arrived, especially from Great Britain and Germany. In more recent times, Chile has welcomed newcomers from Arab countries and other South American nations, especially Bolivia and Peru.

Today's immigrants come to Chile seeking jobs and a better life. Chile is attractive because it has built one of the strongest economies in South America. The country has vast amounts of copper that it sells around the world, and its rich farmlands produce fruits, vegetables, and meat. The country also has a stable, democratic government, though that was not always the case.

In 1973, the country's military took over the government. Under General Augusto Pinochet, the government limited personal freedoms and arrested and killed many Chileans who opposed it. Pinochet's rule ended in 1990, but Chileans still remember those harsh years.

Chileans are proud of their country and its success. The people believe in staying close to their families and working hard. Chileans welcome visitors who come to explore the country's great natural beauty. Chile offers these guests beautiful beaches, fantastic ski slopes, and spectacular scenery at every turn. Chileans enjoy this beauty, too—and the knowledge that they live in a peaceful, growing nation.

Visitors view the colorful formations in the Valley of the Moon, part of the Atacama Desert of northern Chile.

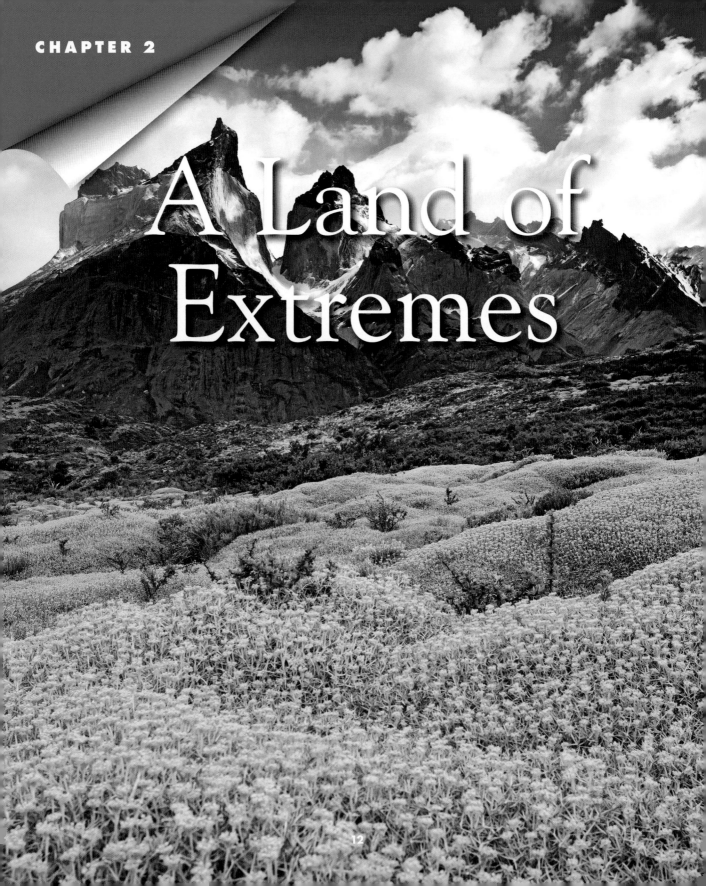

CHAPTER 2

A Land of Extremes

O N A MAP, CHILE LOOKS LIKE A LONG STRIP OF land clinging to the western edge of South America. At a length of 2,654 miles (4,270 kilometers), it stretches farther north to south than any other country in the world. That great length contrasts with the nation's width. On average, Chile is only about 110 miles (177 km) wide. The country's total area is 291,930 square miles (756,100 sq km), making it a little larger than the U.S. state of Texas.

The Lay of the Land

Chile's entire western border is the Pacific Ocean. Peru lies to the north, Bolivia to the northeast, and Argentina to the east. The Andes Mountains run down the eastern edge of Chile and include many active volcanoes. Activity beneath the earth's surface causes volcanic eruptions. That activity also creates earthquakes. Both are caused by the shifting of tectonic plates, which are giant pieces of rock that make up earth's surface. A quake that hit near Valdivia, Chile, in 1960 had a magnitude of 9.5, making it the most powerful earthquake ever recorded. It killed about 1,600 people.

Chile's territory includes thousands of islands. The largest is Tierra del Fuego, which Chile shares with Argentina. The island sits across the Strait of Magellan, a narrow body of water that connects the Pacific and Atlantic Oceans. Other important islands belonging to Chile include Easter Island, Chiloé Island, and the Juan Fernández Islands. Easter Island is far from

Chile's 1960 earthquake left much of Valdivia in ruins. The earthquake also set off tsunamis, large ocean waves that devastated coastlines, leaving two million people homeless.

Chile, 2,220 miles (3,570 km) away in the Pacific. Also far from shore is the land Chile claims in Antarctica, about 600 miles (965 km) south of Chile. Like other nations, Chile has several military and research bases on the frozen continent.

The Northern Regions

Chile has five major geographic regions. Farthest north is the Norte Grande, or Great North. The dominant landscape in this region is the Atacama Desert, the driest desert in the world. The desert is covered with rocks and sand. The region also has salt pans—flat areas covered with salt. These are dotted with small bodies of water called lagoons. The Norte Grande holds much of Chile's minerals, especially copper, a valuable metal.

Chile's Geographic Features

Area: 291,930 square miles (756,100 sq km)

Highest Elevation: Ojos del Salado, 22,572 feet (6,880 m)

Lowest Elevation: Sea level along the coast

Longest River: Loa, 275 miles (440 km)

Largest Lake: General Carrera (shared with Argentina), 714 square miles (1,850 sq km)

Highest Lake: Ojos del Salado crater lake, 20,964 feet (6,390 m)

Average High Temperature: In Santiago, 85°F (29°C) in January; 58°F (14°C) in July

Average Low Temperature: In Santiago, 53°F (12°C) in January; 37°F (3°C) in July

Highest Average Annual Precipitation: About 200 inches (500 cm), at the Strait of Magellan

Lowest Average Annual Precipitation: Arica, 0.03 inches (0.08 cm)

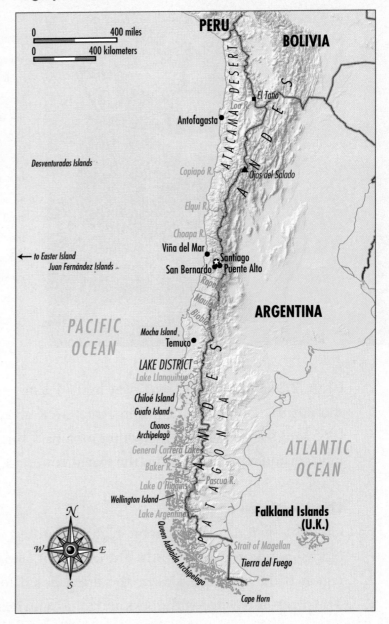

Along the Pacific Coast are fine beaches, and most people in the region live close to the water. Moving inland the land begins to rise, and a small mountain range starts and runs south through most of the country. The peaks can reach 7,000 feet (2,100 meters). Moving east toward the Andes, the land continues to rise, reaching an elevation of about 11,000 feet (3,350 m) in a region called the *altiplano* (high plain).

In the Norte Grande, several countries have built huge observatories to study the stars. The region's dry conditions and high elevation make the air very clear. The region's sparse population means that there is little light pollution. Together, these qualities make the region perfect for scientific observation.

The Norte Grande is also home to Chile's longest river. The U-shaped Loa River travels 275 miles (440 km) as it flows from the Andes to the Pacific. The river supports plants that bring patches of green to a mostly desert region.

The waves of the Pacific Ocean lap against the rocky land in Antofagasta, in northern Chile. The action of the waves and wind have eroded some of the rock into an arch known as La Portada, "the gateway."

Stirrings Below the Earth

Hot water from beneath the earth sometimes reaches the surface, creating hot springs. Other times, however, the water can't freely escape, and instead, steam and sometimes hot water shoot through cracks or small holes in the earth's surface. This is a geyser.

In the Norte Grande Andes sits El Tatio, the highest field of geysers in the world at 13,800 feet (4,200 m). It's also the largest geyser field in the Southern Hemisphere. El Tatio has more than eighty active geysers. Visitors must walk carefully, as the ground is thin in spots, and people have been known to fall into hot water below.

South of the Norte Grande is the Norte Chico, or Little North. It runs from just south of the city of Antofagasta to just north of Santiago. The Norte Chico is not as dry as the Norte Grande. Melting snow from the Andes helps feed small rivers such as the Elqui and Choapa. In the surrounding valley, Chileans raise crops and cattle. The grapes of the region are used to make *pisco*, an alcoholic beverage enjoyed across Chile. In the Andes of the Norte Chico is the country's tallest peak, Ojos del Salado, which rises to 22,572 feet (6,880 m). It is the world's tallest active volcano.

Valle Central

The middle region of Chile is called the Valle Central, or Central Valley. It starts just north of Santiago and extends down to the Biobío River, Chile's second-longest river. It once marked the boundary between colonial Chile and the lands of the Mapuche.

The Cities of Chile

Chile's capital, Santiago, is the largest city in Chile, with an estimated population of 5,128,041 in 2014. Both the second-largest and fourth-largest cities in Chile are suburbs of Santiago. Puente Alto is home to about 802,000 people, while San Bernardo has a population of roughly 316,000.

Antofagasta (below), in the north, is Chile's third-largest city with a population of about 391,000. Ships leave its port with copper and other minerals. The British once played a major role in business here, and the city has a clock that looks like London's Big Ben.

Viña del Mar (Vineyard of the Sea) is home to about 288,000. The city is sometimes called the Garden City because of its many public parks. The city also hosts Chile's largest musical festival each year, the International Song Festival. Musicians come from across Latin America to take part.

The southern city of Temuco has a population of about 265,000. The city was founded in 1881 to administer territory taken from the Mapuche. The city has grown quickly in recent years. Its Regional Museum of Araucanía explores the history and culture of the indigenous peoples of the south.

About 250,000 people live in Valparaíso (above). The city has a long history as a major port. Valparaíso is known for its steep hills and the stairways leading up them. Residents also ride small railways called funiculars up some hills. Valparaíso is a colorful city, with street art painted on many buildings.

Unlike the drier north, the Valle Central is filled with many productive farms. It is also home to most of Chile's residents, who enjoy easy access to both beautiful beaches and Andean ski resorts.

Southern Regions

Moving south, the next region in Chile is called the Sur—the South. The area was heavily forested until Chile defeated the Mapuche and took control of the region in 1881. Then settlers from Europe moved in. They cleared many of the trees

Workers cut grass that will be used as cattle feed on a farm in the Valle Central.

Hikers trek across the rugged landscape in Patagonia.

and began raising cattle. Today, tree farming is its major economic activity. The Sur is the home of the Lake District, an area in the mountains with many lakes. Llanquihue, Chile's second-largest lake, is in this region.

Off the coast of the Sur is the island of Chiloé, one of the largest islands in South America. Chiloé is home to rich temperate rain forests and abundant wildlife, and many tourists come to explore its national parks.

The last of Chile's five major regions is the Zona Austral, or Southern Zone. Chile reaches its narrowest width here, just 40 miles (64 km) across. The region includes Chile's portion of Patagonia and most of Chile's islands. Patagonia has few full-time residents, but its natural beauty attracts visitors. Just over half of Chilean Patagonia is protected by the government to preserve the wilderness. The region has

Beautiful rock formations known as the Marble Cathedral rise above the water of General Carrera Lake.

fjords—narrow waterways that cut through steep cliffs, and slow-moving fields of ice called glaciers. In the Patagonian Andes is General Carrera Lake, Chile's largest lake, which it shares with Argentina. The region also has Baker River, the country's widest river. Off the shore of Patagonia is Tierra del Fuego, and south of that is Cape Horn, where the Atlantic and Pacific Oceans meet.

Climate

Given Chile's diverse landscapes, it is no surprise that the climate also varies greatly. Since Chile sits below the equator, its seasons are reversed from those in North America. Summer begins in December and lasts until March, while winter runs from June to September.

In the Norte Grande, parts of the Atacama Desert go years without rain. In 2015, some areas were hit with rare thunderstorms, and more rain fell in one day than usually falls over several years. The downpour led to floods in the city of Antofagasta and

Rust-colored ridges break up the flat land in the Atacama Desert. In some parts of the desert, rain has never been measured.

other parts of the region. Rain is more common in the altiplano during the summer. The coast might see rain, but most moisture there comes as fog that rolls in off the ocean.

Temperatures in the Norte Grande vary widely. Daytime temperatures in the desert can reach well over 86 degrees Fahrenheit (30 degrees Celsius) while falling to below freezing at night. Along the coast, the temperatures generally stay

A skier heads down the steep Andean slopes in Portillo, in central Chile.

Catching the Fog

Like the Norte Grande, the coast of the Norte Chico sees plenty of fog. This moisture helps plants grow. It can also serve as a source of drinking water for people who live in otherwise dry areas. Around Coquimbo, scientists have been testing a system to collect the water in fog and use it for drinking. The system being used in Chile looks something like a giant window screen. The wind moves through the tiny holes in the screen, but the water is trapped and then collected. The system collects more water than other fog-trapping inventions, and the scientists hope that one day it will provide drinking water for remote villages in the driest parts of Chile.

in the range of 59°F (15°C) and 77°F (25°C). In the Norte Chico, more rain falls, especially during the winter, and temperatures are slightly lower than in the Norte Grande.

The Valle Central has what is called a Mediterranean climate. Rains come in the winter and the temperatures are comfortable, while the summers are hot and dry. Snow sometimes falls in the region's mountains.

Chile's southern zones receive the most rain. Some areas get 200 inches (500 centimeters) of precipitation every year. Temperatures are usually moderate along the coast but get colder farther inland and south. The climate varies widely in Patagonia. Some parts have strong winds and more moisture, while closer to the Andes the climate is dry and cold. In the southern part of Patagonia, the temperature in summer averages 51°F (10.6°C) and just 36°F (2°C) in winter.

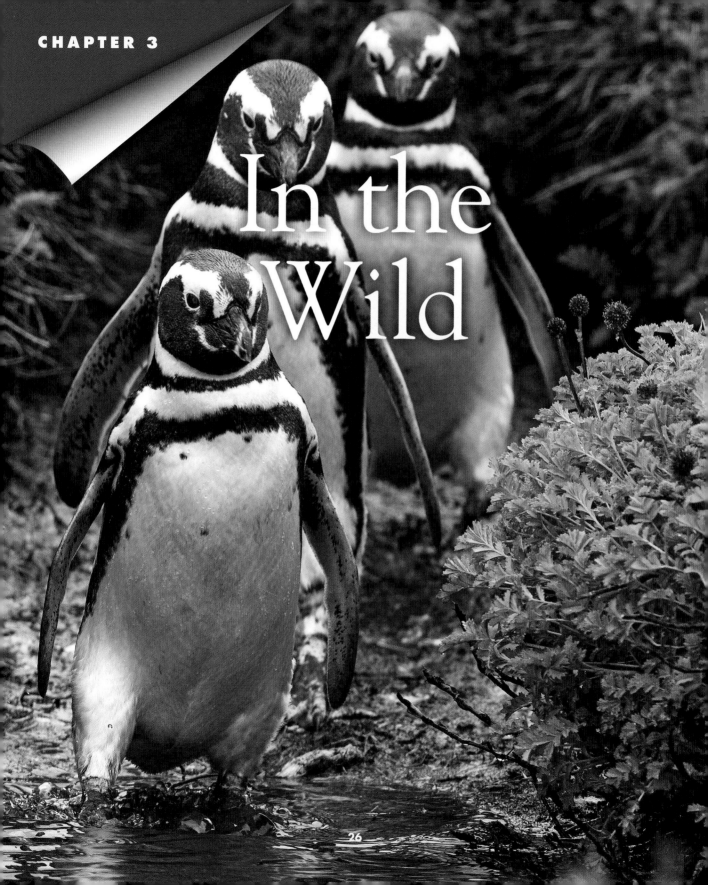

CHAPTER 3

In the Wild

CHILE'S VARIED LANDSCAPES AND CLIMATES HAVE given rise to a remarkable diversity of wildlife. The animals range from desert dwellers that have adapted to the dryness to penguins that live on islands along the wet Strait of Magellan.

In the North

Living in one of the driest places on earth is not easy, but wildlife can be found in the Atacama Desert. Mammals are rare there, though some fox and mice live in scattered areas. The region is home to a larger number of insects, scorpions, and reptiles. In some spots, clouds and mountains combine to create areas of fog. The moisture in the fog allows some plants to grow. The areas where this happens are called *lomas*. Hundreds of different plants live in the lomas, and many of them are endemic to Chile, meaning they're found nowhere else on earth. The lomas also attract some birds, including several kinds of hummingbirds and the Peruvian song sparrow.

Opposite: **Three Magellanic penguins march toward the water near Otway Sound, in Chilean Patagonia. Magellanic penguins, which live about twenty years, mate for life.**

In the Wild **27**

Parts of the Atacama Desert burst into spectacular bloom in 2015, after a record-setting rain.

When rain finally comes to the desert, parts of the Atacama burst into color. Seeds from such flowers as the *pata de guanaco* and the *garra de Leon* that have been buried in the dry earth suddenly come to life. Several years can pass between times when the desert flowers.

The coastal regions in the north are home to seagulls, pelicans, and other seabirds. The animal residents of the altiplano include several relatives of the camel. For example, over the centuries, llamas have been tamed and used as pack animals. The much smaller alpacas and vicuñas are known for their soft wool, which can be used for clothing. The vicuña faced extinction several decades ago, but government protection has helped the numbers rise to about twenty-five thousand by 2015. The Aymara, an indigenous group in the north, catch some vicuña to shear them for their wool. Then they release the animals back into the wild.

Other mammals of the north's mountainous regions include the taruca, a relative of the deer, and the viscacha, a rodent with a long tail and large ears. Higher up in the mountains lives the chinchilla, another rodent. Chinchillas have extremely soft fur, and scientists once thought they had been hunted to extinction. But during the 1970s, some were discovered in central Chile. The altiplano and Andes in northern Chile are home to two kinds of wildcats. Pumas are the second-largest cats from the Americas. Much smaller is the colocolo, which is

Pumas live from northern Canada to the southern tip of South America. No other wild, large land mammal in the Americas has such an extensive range.

On Top of the World

Lauca National Park covers a large area in the high plains and the Andes. In places, the park's elevation rises above 20,000 feet (6,100 m). The park is home to many kinds of mammals, including pumas, tarucas, and alpacas. One of its most notable plants is the queñoa. No other tree in the world grows at such high elevations.

about the size of a house cat. Birds found in the Norte Grande's higher elevations include ducks, eagles, condors, and rheas. A relative of the ostrich, the rhea cannot fly but is a fast runner. Flamingos come to the region's high lakes. Some also breed at the lagoons found at lower elevations.

A rhea rests on the ground at Torres del Paine National Park. Male rheas incubate the eggs, keeping them warm for about forty days until they are ready to hatch.

The wetter Norte Chico supports a greater variety of wild-life than the far north. Chile's largest rodent, the coipo, lives in the southern end of the region and into the Valle Central. It spends much of its time in water.

Along the coast, Fray Jorge National Park is home to sea otters, viscachas, and eagles. Off the coast, Humboldt National Reserve covers three islands. Humboldt penguins nest on

An otter emerges from sea near Chiloe Island carrying a crab, one of its most common foods.

National Flower

Chile's national flower is the copihue, which grows on vines in forests in the central part of the country. These vines can grow to be 30 feet (9 m) tall. The copihue is sometimes called the bellflower, because of its shape. The plant's fruit is edible and its roots can be used to make medicine, but cutting and selling wild copihues is against the law.

A male Darwin's frog with its young. These frogs live along forest streams in Chile and Argentina.

these islands and other islands farther south. Bottlenose dolphins swim in the waters around the islands. Fish found in these and other Chilean waters include tuna and sole. Farther south, fishers catch Chilean sea bass.

In the Valle Central

Large parts of the Valle Central have been developed for farms and cities, but many kinds of wildlife survive in the region. In the forests live foxes, rabbits, and a type of skunk called a chingue. One rare mammal of the region is the kodkod, the world's smallest wildcat. Another type of cat, the pampas cat, lives in the mountains of central Chile. Both of these cats come out at night to hunt small animals and birds. One animal that is food for the kodkod is a rodent called the degu.

Hundreds of degus live together underground. If a wildcat or other predator grabs its tail, a degu spins around until the tail skin tears off. Then it can pull away and flee.

Birds of the central region include the giant hummingbird. At up to 8 inches (20 cm) long, it's the largest hummingbird in the world. The Valle Central is home to several kinds of parrots. The burrowing parrot builds its nest inside cracks found in cliffs. The birds often build nests together to create large colonies. Near some of the region's lakes live black-necked swans and other waterbirds. Fish in these lakes include a type of mackerel called the *pejerrey chileno*. A well-known frog of the region is Darwin's frog. After the female frog lays eggs, the male frog helps nurture its young by keeping the eggs and then the tadpoles in its mouth. Once the tadpoles turn into tiny frogs, they hop out of their father's mouth.

Saving Sea Life

A large variety of wildlife lives along Chile's coast and in ocean waters. This includes whales, squid, sea lions, tuna, and penguins. To protect some of the sea life off the coast of the Valle Central, Chile announced in 2015 the creation of the Nazca-Desventuradas Marine Park. The park will be the largest of its kind in the Western Hemisphere. Creating the park will help protect such creatures as giant lobsters, deep-sea sharks, and the Juan Fernández fur seal, once thought to be extinct. Another marine park off Easter Island will also protect the sea life there, though the Rapa Nui, the indigenous people of the island, will still be allowed to fish in nearby waters.

The plant life of the Valle Central includes some unusual trees. The monkey puzzle tree got its name because its sharp branches and hard leaves would puzzle a monkey trying to safely climb it. In 1990, Chile declared the monkey puzzle tree a national monument, making it a crime to cut one down. Even so, some are illegally cut down to make way for farms. The Chilean wine palm tree was once common in the region, but its numbers diminished after Spanish settlers cut it down for its sweet sap. As with the monkey puzzle tree, the Chilean government has set aside forests where the wine palm tree is protected. The Chilean palm is a huge tree. It can reach a height of 90 feet (27 m) and a width of 5 feet (1.5 m). Some of these trees live to be hundreds of years old.

Orange flowers stand out against the green spiny leaves of the monkey puzzle tree.

In the South

Tens of thousands of years ago, huge sheets of ice covered much of North and South America. Part of southern Chile was one of the few areas that stayed ice-free. The warmer temperatures enabled wildlife that died in other regions to survive in Chile.

Southern Chile is home to one of the world's few temperate rain forests. Like rain forests in tropical climates, a temperate rain forest gets plenty of rain, but temperatures are not as hot year-round. The wildlife there includes the giant otter, which can reach 5 feet (1.5 m) in length. At barely 18 inches (46 cm) tall, the southern pudu is the world's smallest deer. Another tiny mammal found here is the *monito del monte*, or little mountain monkey, a creature barely bigger than a mouse. It is actually a marsupial, a creature that carries its young in its pouch. The Magellanic woodpecker, South

Many of the rocks and trees in Chile's temperate rain forest are covered with moss.

America's largest woodpecker, grows up to 18 inches (46 cm) long and is endemic in Chile's rain forest.

Along the coast, rock cormorants raise their young on cliffs or jetties near the water. One rare tree along the coast is the *alerce*, which can live for several thousand years. Shingles made from its bark are resistant to rain. The *murta*, a bush found in the south, produces berries used to make jelly.

Chile's most southern region, the Zona Austral, is a harsh land with a harsh climate. Yet, as in the desert, some wildlife thrives there. Mammals include pumas and guanacos. The Magellanic penguin is found here as well as farther north. Other birds of the region include albatrosses and ducks. Trees that live in the south include the lenga tree, a type of beech, which has leaves that change colors as fall approaches. Another Chilean beech, the coihue, stays green year-round.

National Animal

Chile's national animal is the huemul, a rugged deer relative that lives in Chile's southern mountains. Some say the huemul is more like a mountain goat than a deer, as it can easily scramble over rocky ground. The huemul has short legs and thick fur. It appears on the Chilean coat of arms, one of the official symbols of the government, along with an Andean condor.

The waters off the Zona Austral, extending down to Antarctica, are filled with wildlife ranging from tiny krill to giant blue whales, which eat krill by the ton every day. Many seals and sea lions live near the coast.

Island Wildlife

Many of Chile's endemic wildlife species live on its major islands. The Juan Fernández Islands, for example, are home to about one hundred endemic plants and animals. One of these is the Juan Fernández firecrown, a hummingbird found on just one island in the group.

The island of Chiloé is home to penguins and is the winter resting spot for several species of birds. Thousands of Hudsonian godwits fly there from Alaska every year. Tierra del Fuego, along with other parts of the Zona Austral, is home to the Magellanic lizard, the most southerly reptile in South America. The only native animals on Easter Island, the farthest island from the Chilean mainland, are some small lizards and insects. The mammals on the island, including rats, traveled there with settlers long ago.

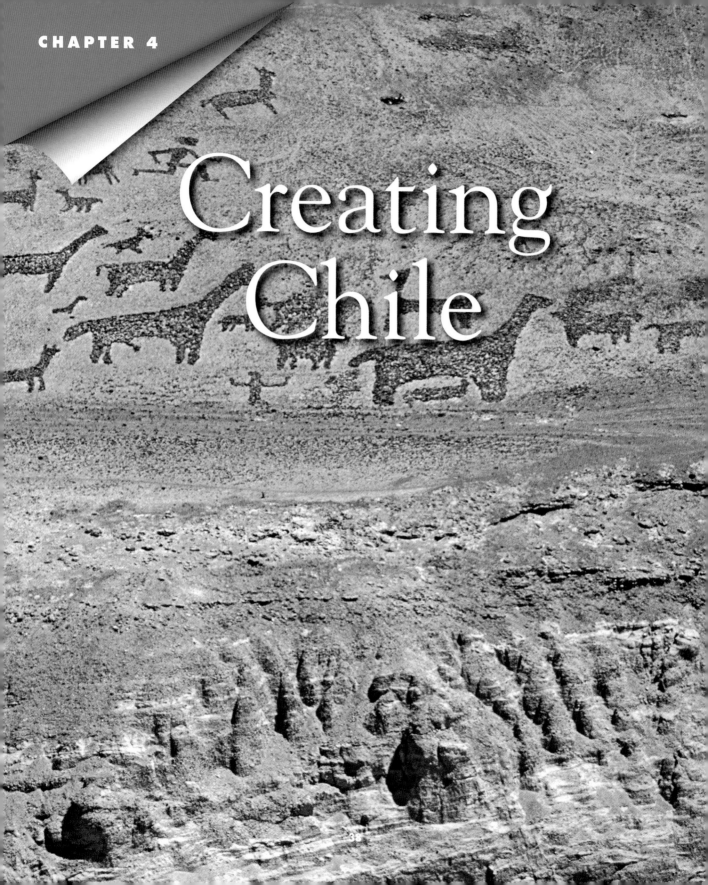

CHAPTER 4

Creating
Chile

THE FIRST PEOPLE KNOWN TO HAVE SETTLED IN SOUTH America lived at the southern end of Chile. They lived at a site called Monte Verde, and it dates back nearly fifteen thousand years. From Monte Verde, Chile's residents slowly spread across the land between the ocean and the Andes. Those who lived along the coast collected shellfish. Inland the people hunted mammals and gathered wild fruit.

Opposite: **Long ago, people in northern Chile made giant pictures in the desert. These pictures include dozens of images of llamas and alpacas.**

Early Peoples

An early group of settlers was the Chinchorro, who came to northern Chile around 6000 BCE. They lived along the coast in small villages. Today, they are known for the mummies they left behind, which are the oldest in the world. Unlike the ancient Egyptians, who mummified only kings and other powerful people, the Chinchorro mummified all their dead.

A Danger to the Mummies

The first Chinchorro mummies were found in the Atacama Desert in 1917. Over the centuries, the dry climate there preserved the mummies. Now, however, the climate in the desert is becoming slightly more humid, which could be related to global changes in the climate. Today, the mummies found in the desert are often blemished and falling apart. Even mummies kept in museums are turning black. The problem has been linked to bacteria, tiny microorganisms. The extra moisture in the Atacama region makes it easier for the bacteria to live on the mummies' skin. The bacteria eat the skin, causing the mummies to decay.

Other early peoples in northern Chile, dating back to centuries after the Chinchorro, created large images in the earth called geoglyphs. Some are carved in the ground while others are made of layers of dirt and stone. The largest of the geoglyphs is called the Atacama Giant. The picture is 282 feet (86 m) tall.

Some time after 600 CE, the people of northern Chile learned how to farm. Their crops included corn, beans, potatoes, and cotton. The people built stone houses around their farms, creating villages.

The first Chilean farmers were a people known today as the Diaguita. Farther south lived the Mapuche, which means "people of the land." They relied on farming for most of their food and raised llama for wool. The Mapuche were split into smaller groups and worked together to defend themselves.

Around 1470, the different Mapuche groups united to hold off an invasion by the Inca. Originally from Peru, the Inca built an empire that spread into what are now Bolivia, Colombia, Argentina, and Ecuador. The Inca managed to gain control of Chile as far south as the site of Santiago before the Mapuche stopped their advance. After the war, the Mapuche sometimes traded with the Inca. In the north, the Inca forced the local people to farm and mine for them.

Europeans Arrive

Portuguese explorer Ferdinand Magellan was sailing for Spain when he passed by Tierra del Fuego in 1520, through the strait that now bears his name. His voyage was part of the competition between the nations of Europe to explore the world and build colonies. In these colonies, European rulers hoped to acquire gold, spices, and other natural resources.

Spain came to dominate most of Central and South America. The first Spaniard to reach Chile was Diego de Almagro. He was a conquistador, a soldier who helped Spain conquer lands in the Americas. In 1532, Almagro fought the Inca in Peru, and three years later he traveled to Chile looking

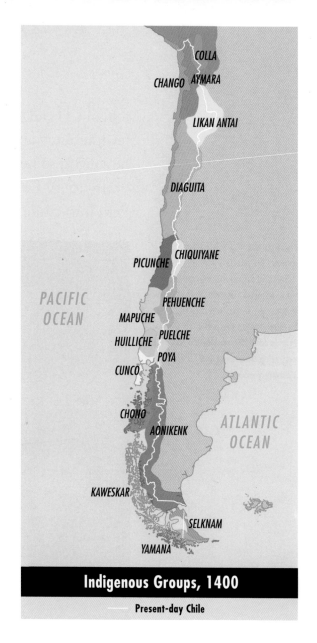

Indigenous Groups, 1400

—— Present-day Chile

for gold. He angered the local people when he demanded they feed his army and work for him. Almagro didn't find the gold he sought, so he returned to Peru.

In 1540, Pedro de Valdivia led another expedition from Peru into Chile. Like Almagro, he forced the local people to

Pedro de Valdivia first came to South America in 1534, acting as second in command under Francisco Pizarro, who attacked the indigenous people in Peru. He went on to serve as the royal governor of Chile for seven years.

Many Spanish soldiers traveled to the Americas as conquistadores. They hoped to find wealth for their homeland as well as themselves. In Chile, Inés de Suarez (1507–1580) was the rare woman who helped the men in their conquests. She was a conquistadora. Suarez first came to Peru to join her husband, who was a soldier. After he died, Suarez began a relationship with Pedro de Valdivia and went with him to Chile. When the local people attacked Santiago, Suarez is said to have taken a sword, jumped on a horse, and helped lead the defense of the village. Suarez later married another Chilean soldier and remained in Chile until her death. In 2006, the Chilean writer Isabel Allende published *Inés of My Soul*, a novel describing some of the details of Suarez's life.

work for him. Valdivia stopped at a spot he called Santiago, which became Spain's first permanent settlement in Chile. Angry at how Valdivia had treated them, the local people attacked the settlement but were unable to conquer the fort. The Spanish rebuilt Santiago and put it and their farms under constant guard. But Valdivia was more interested in gold than crops, and he forced the local people to mine for it.

Building a Colony

Valdivia became the first Spanish governor of Chile. He reported to Spanish leaders in Peru, who took their orders from Spain's King Charles V. In Chile, Valdivia introduced the *encomienda*, a system used in other Spanish lands. Under this system, a Spanish master controlled all the indigenous people on his lands and could force them to work in mines or on farms. The masters were supposed to treat the indigenous people well and teach them Christianity. But most Spanish masters treated the Mapuche and others badly, causing strife between the native groups and the Spanish.

From Santiago, Valdivia set out to start new settlements.

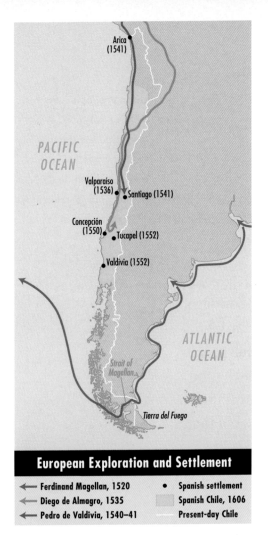

PACIFIC OCEAN

Arica (1541)

Valparaiso (1536)
Santiago (1541)

Concepción (1550)
Tucapel (1552)

Valdivia (1552)

ATLANTIC OCEAN

Strait of Magellan

Tierra del Fuego

European Exploration and Settlement

← Ferdinand Magellan, 1520
← Diego de Almagro, 1535
← Pedro de Valdivia, 1540–41

• Spanish settlement
  Spanish Chile, 1606
  Present-day Chile

The town of Concepción was founded in 1550, and a town named Valdivia was established two years later. As Spanish settlers moved south, they brought the encomienda system with them, angering the Mapuche who were forced to work for them. Some Mapuche managed to steal Spanish horses and form their own small cavalry. Then in 1553, the Mapuche and other native people rebelled against the Spanish. They attacked a fort called Tucapel, killing all the soldiers stationed there. The indigenous forces captured Valdivia and later executed him.

The Mapuche tried to attack Santiago, but the Spanish defeated them. After this battle, the Spanish stopped pushing southward into Mapuche lands. They focused on strengthening their control where they had already settled.

Rebel Leader

A Mapuche leader named Caupolicán was at the center of the 1553 rebellion. Known for his physical strength, Caupolicán was chosen to command Mapuche forces against the Spanish. He worked with Lautaro, a former servant of Pedro de Valdivia who had learned Spanish methods of fighting before returning to his people. After capturing Valdivia in Tucapel, Caupolicán served as a judge at a trial that led to the governor's execution for his treatment of the Mapuche. Caupolicán continued battling the Spanish until they caught him in 1558. They executed him for being a rebel.

A Growing Colony

By the start of the seventeenth century, about ten thousand Spaniards lived in Chile. Because of disease and war, the indigenous population had fallen from about one million to five hundred thousand. Most of those who survived were Mapuche living in the south. The Spanish called the Mapuche and other indigenous people of the south *Araucanos*, or Southern people.

The Spanish bought African slaves to work on farms, but Chile had fewer enslaved people than other South American colonies. Many of the workers who were not enslaved were *mestizos*—children from parents of different ethnic or racial backgrounds.

Chilean society, like Spanish society, had distinct classes. The colony's rulers were from Spain. The next highest social class was the *criollos*—people of Spanish descent born in

The Mapuche fought to maintain their independence from the Spanish and were largely successful for several hundred years.

Chile. The mestizos were below them, and enslaved Africans and indigenous people were in the lowest class.

Chile did not appear to have huge amounts of gold, silver, or other valuable resources. Farming was its main economic activity through the seventeenth century. Chile's leaders had a good deal of freedom to do what they liked, since their capital was so far from government officials in Peru and Spain. Still, the Spanish government tried to control life in Chile as much as it could. It said foreigners could not settle there. It also forced all goods to go through Panama to make it easier to collect taxes on them. Some of that money paid for a large army Spain kept in Chile because it feared Mapuche uprisings and foreign attacks. One foreign attack occurred in 1578 when the English pirate and explorer Sir Francis Drake sacked Valparaíso. The coast saw more English attacks a century later.

During the eighteenth century, some foreigners did settle in the colony. One of them was Ambrosio O'Higgins, who came to Chile from Ireland and became governor of Chile in 1788. As governor, O'Higgins ended the encomienda system, tried to improve the mining industry, and promoted business.

The Battle for Independence

In the early nineteenth century, events in Spain greatly affected Chile. In 1808, Napoleon Bonaparte of France invaded Spain. He later forced King Charles IV to give up the throne. In Chile, the most powerful criollos remained loyal to Fernando, the son of Charles. They decided to rule themselves until he could regain power, and they created a new government in 1810.

Some Chileans wanted to cut all ties with Spain and be completely independent. This group was led by José Miguel Carrera and his brothers, who took control of the government in 1811. Their sister, Javiera, aided them and is said to have designed the first flag for an independent Chile. The Carerras' rule was brief, however, as Spanish troops and their Chilean supporters battled to regain control. The fighting lasted until 1814, when the Spanish defeated the rebels.

The rebels had made several important changes during their rule. They ended slavery and created an elected government. After Spain regained control of Chile, it ended these reforms, causing more Chileans to support independence from Spain. Some joined with Argentine troops who also wanted to end Spanish rule in South America. In 1817, Argentine general José de San Martín, together with Chilean patriot Bernardo O'Higgins, led an army of Argentines and exiled Chileans into Chile and defeated the troops loyal to Spain.

Bernardo O'Higgins (1778–1842) was the son of Ambrosio O'Higgins and a Chilean woman who came from a wealthy Spanish family. He studied for a time in Spain and England before returning home to run his father's farm. As early as 1810, Bernardo O'Higgins wanted total independence from Spain. In 1813, while battling Chileans who supported Spain, he encouraged his troops by shouting, "Live with honor or die with glory! He who is brave, follow me!" O'Higgins won that battle, but the next year he and his men were forced to flee to Argentina. In 1817, O'Higgins returned to Chile and helped win the war for independence. He was named the new country's supreme director, which is like a president. Today, O'Higgins is considered Chile's national hero.

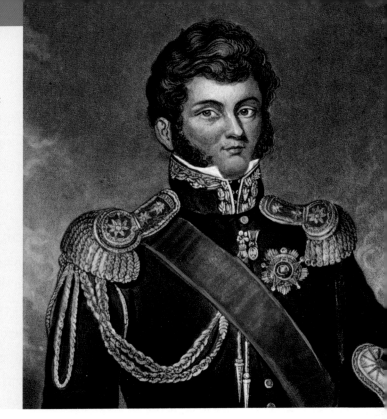

This victory ensured Chile's independence, which was officially declared the next year.

The Nation of Chile

Bernardo O'Higgins became Chile's head of state. Trying to make Chile a more modern country, he started colleges, libraries, and hospitals and raised taxes to pay for these improvements. But some wealthy Chileans and leaders of the Roman Catholic Church wanted things as they had been under Spanish rule. This group, known as conservatives, wanted to remain in control of the country. They opposed O'Higgins and forced him out of power in 1823. Through the rest of the decade, the conservatives and people who opposed them struggled to control the government.

Finally, in 1830, Diego Portales emerged as Chile's new leader. He called for a new constitution, which gave the conservative landowners most of the power in Chile. The constitution said the president could pick the men who ran for Congress, the part of government that created laws. These men usually did as the president wanted. Political rights were severely limited, because only men who owned a certain amount of property could vote.

Portales's changes limited democracy but brought order to the country and made it possible to defend against the Mapuche and their Spanish allies to the south. Chile's economy also began to grow. Copper and silver mining became a major industry, and Valparaíso, a city to the north of Santiago, became an important trading center. Ships from all over the world entered its harbor. Immigrants from Germany and other parts of Europe started to settle in the south. Many farmworkers moved to growing towns to look for work, and the government built several thousand schools. By 1851, Chile had built the first railway system in South America, and a telegraph line followed. British and U.S. investors helped pay for some of these improvements, helping Chile become the most modern nation on the continent.

Despite Chile's growth, many residents were not happy with their government. They wanted a greater say in how the country was run. In 1851, a civil war broke out and several thousand people died in the fighting. President Manuel Montt ended the rebellion with help from Great Britain. Montt was the last powerful conservative president of the era, as those seeking reform, called liberals, slowly gained power in the government. In 1874, Chile said all adult males could vote, ending the previous property requirement. Radicals, people who sought even greater change and more power for average Chileans, also emerged to challenge the liberals and conservatives.

Battling Neighbors

As Chileans built their nation, they battled neighboring countries. During the 1830s, Peru and Bolivia united briefly. Chile already had trade disagreements with Peru, and it feared the united power of the two countries. Chile declared war on the new union in 1836. Its troops won a major victory in 1839 and forced Bolivia and Peru to separate.

Valparaíso in 1840. The city, one of Chile's largest, thrived despite pirate attacks, earthquakes, and devastating fires.

A copper and silver works from 1820. Mining has long been central to Chile's economy.

During the 1860s, Chile's relations with Bolivia became tense as they argued over their border in the Atacama Desert. Then, in 1879, disputes over taxing mining led to war between the two countries, with Peru coming to Bolivia's aid. This so-called War of the Pacific lasted until 1884. Despite having a smaller military than its enemies, Chile won and took land from both Bolivia and Peru.

During this time the Chilean government also battled the Mapuche. Like Spain before it, Chile had not tried to move south into Mapuche lands, but by the mid-nineteenth century some Chilean settlers and soldiers did begin to move in. In 1881, the Mapuche attacked the forts and towns around them, but the Chilean military was stronger and defeated them. The Chileans took over most Mapuche lands, and the Mapuche began a long struggle to receive fair treatment.

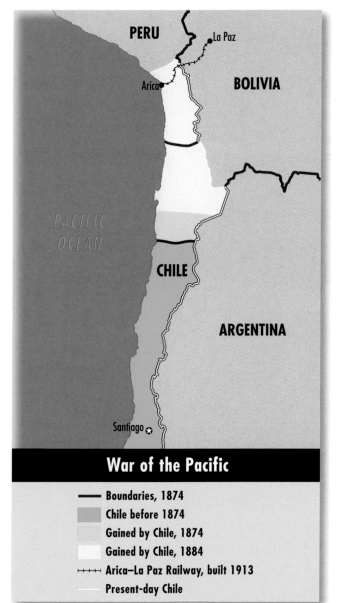

War of the Pacific

— Boundaries, 1874
▨ Chile before 1874
▨ Gained by Chile, 1874
▨ Gained by Chile, 1884
┼┼┼┼ Arica–La Paz Railway, built 1913
— Present-day Chile

Challenges in a New Century

The lands Chile acquired after winning the War of the Pacific led to new wealth. The new territory had valuable nitrate mines. Chile sold nitrate, which was used in fertilizer and gunpowder, around the world. The mines in the north attracted workers from all over the country. So did the growing cities of Santiago, Valparaíso, Concepción, and Valdivia, where factories produced clothing, food, and other goods.

Chile's ruling class controlled all parts of society, while many average Chileans faced bad living conditions. By the 1900s, workers in the mines and factories were clamoring for a better life. Miners began forming unions, organizations of workers that would fight for higher pay and better working conditions. To win their demands for better pay, union members sometimes went on strike, refusing to work. In

When the War of the Pacific ended in 1884, Bolivia and Chile agreed to sign a treaty of peace and friendship. But it wasn't until 1904 that they actually completed the treaty, which called for the construction of a railroad from Arica, Chile, to the Bolivian capital of La Paz. Chile had won Bolivia's coastal region in the war, and the railroad would give Bolivia access to the Pacific Ocean.

After seven years of construction, the railroad opened in 1913. It is one of the world's highest lines, rising to almost 14,000 feet (4,250 m). Over the years, floods washed out parts of the track, and Bolivia accused Chile of not repairing some of the track in its territory. Today, highways make it easier for Bolivia to bring goods to the coast by truck. But to Bolivians, the railroad is a reminder that it lost important land to Chile.

1907, miners went on strike in Iquique. The government sent in troops, who fired at miners and their families. At least five hundred people were killed or wounded. Violence sometimes broke out during later strikes. Miners faced additional problems after scientists learned how to make artificial nitrate. The nitrate mines began to close, putting miners out of work.

In 1920, average Chileans helped elect Arturo Alessandri president. Alessandri tried to make changes to help his supporters, but conservatives opposed him. He did manage to create a new constitution, which balanced powers more equally between the president and Congress.

During the 1930s, like most of the world, Chile suffered from the effects of a severe economic downturn called the Great Depression. During this time, businesses closed and thousands of Chileans lost their jobs. World War II (1939–1945) helped pull the world out of the Depression, as countries spent money to build their militaries. Chile stayed neutral during the war, as it had during World War I (1914–1918). But the country contributed to the war effort by selling its copper.

Meanwhile it was also developing close business ties to the United States. That relationship upset some Chilean radicals, who favored socialism. Under this economic system, the government owns most factories. Other radicals supported communism, which favored even more government owner-ship of property and a single political party to control the government. In the decades after World War II, conservatives, liberals, and radicals competed to shape the government.

The Road to Political Crisis

Chile experienced some political reforms, such as expanding voting rights to include women. The government hired more workers as it took over some businesses and increased the number of schools. Farming in the Sur expanded, as new settlers arrived to clear forests to raise cattle and grain. Then, during the early 1960s, Chile bought unused land from some wealthy own-ers and gave it to peasants. In 1964, a new party, the Christian Democrats, came to power. The party believed that all Chileans were entitled to food, housing, education, and legal rights.

Chile was one of the few South American countries with a strong democratic system. Voters could choose their leaders from a number of different parties. In 1970, Chileans made history when they elected the first socialist leader on the con-tinent. Salvador Allende became president with the support of different leftist groups and the Christian Democrats.

During the next two years, Allende made many changes. He took over copper mines owned by foreign companies and raised wages. The government also took over farmland, and it did not

stop armed peasants from sometimes taking land on their own. Allende made many enemies with his policies. Conservatives who supported private ownership or property opposed him. So did some Christian Democrats. Some radicals also disliked Allende, because they thought he didn't go far enough. They wanted him to take over even more private companies.

The growing conflicts within Chile led the military to take action. On September 11, 1973, officers told Allende they were seizing power. The officers had the support of the United States, which disliked Allende's socialist policies. The military offered Allende a plane to leave the country. He refused, so the air force bombed the president's home. Allende died during the fighting. A junta, a group of military officers, took over the government. The junta was led by General Augusto Pinochet.

In the coming months, the military government arrested people they thought might challenge their rule. Soldiers tortured

Salvador Allende became Chile's minister of health in 1938 and remained a major figure in government until his death in 1973.

and killed many of them. The bodies of many of the people who died were never found, and they are known today as "the disappeared." More than three thousand Chileans were killed or disappeared.

Pinochet remained in power into the 1980s. During military rule, the government burned books it disliked, limited the actions of unions, and controlled the media. Many Chileans opposed Pinochet's limits on their freedoms, but others welcomed the order he brought to the country. The economy also strengthened for a time, as Chile stressed more private ownership of business. But the changes did not provide jobs for all Chileans who wanted them, and many people remained poor.

Chilean soldiers fire at La Moneda, the presidential palace in Santiago, while overthrowing President Salvador Allende.

In 1988, Chileans voted to decide if Pinochet would remain president for eight more years. They said no, and the next year the country had its first free elections since the early 1970s. The country had successfully restored its democratic tradition. Still, some people remained haunted by the Pinochet years. Many families had lost relatives to the government killings and people had lost their freedoms.

Although Pinochet had left the presidency, he made himself a lifetime member of the Senate, part of Chile's Congress. He also remained in charge of the military until 1998. Later that year, while in Great Britain, Pinochet was arrested for killing Spanish citizens during his first months in power. Instead of going to court in Spain, he was sent back to Chile. Pinochet died in 2006 while still fighting legal battles.

General Augusto Pinochet ruled Chile for sixteen years. During his first three years in power, more than 100,000 people were arrested for political reasons. Tens of thousands of them were tortured.

Successes and Challenges

As a democracy again, Chile elected both Christian Democrats and socialists. Santiago and other cities built modern skyscrapers and had pockets of great wealth. But in parts of the cities and in the countryside, many people remained poor. The presidents who followed Pinochet tried to use economic growth to help reduce poverty. Medical care and housing have improved. The government has also restored legal rights to unions and others who lost them under Pinochet.

More women have also been serving in high levels of government. In 2006, Chileans elected Michelle Bachelet as Chile's first female president. She left office in 2010 but was later elected again, taking office in 2014.

Despite its improvements since the 1970s, Chile has faced many challenges. For example, copper prices have fallen, and the Mapuche have demanded the return of some of their lands. In 2010, the country's mining industry caught the world's attention when thirty-three miners were trapped underground for sixty-nine days. Thankfully, all survived.

Though problems linger, Chile has built a stable democracy and a strong economy. The Chilean tradition of hard work should help its people meet future challenges.

Mapuche people march through the streets of Santiago as part of a protest against their treatment.

CHAPTER 5

A Strong Democracy

CHILE'S CONSTITUTION OUTLINES THE STRUCTURE of the government and spells out basic laws and rights. The country has had several constitutions since it gained independence. The last one was adopted in 1980, though the country has made changes to it since the end of Augusto Pinochet's rule. In 2015, President Michelle Bachelet began the process of writing a new constitution to replace the one created under Pinochet. She said, "The current constitution had its origins in dictatorship and does not reflect the needs of our times."

Making Laws

Chile, like other nations, has three branches in its government. The legislative branch drafts the country's laws. Chile's legislature is called the National Congress. Its members meet in Valparaíso, but most other government activities take place in the capital, Santiago. The National Congress is divided

National Government of Chile

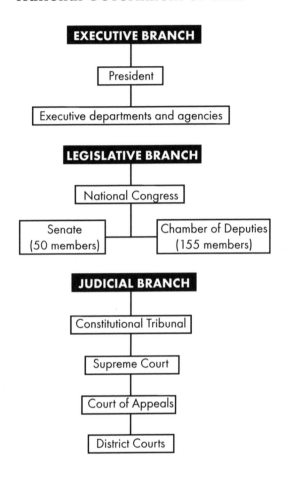

EXECUTIVE BRANCH

President

Executive departments and agencies

LEGISLATIVE BRANCH

National Congress

Senate (50 members)

Chamber of Deputies (155 members)

JUDICIAL BRANCH

Constitutional Tribunal

Supreme Court

Court of Appeals

District Courts

into the Chamber of Deputies and the Senate. A law passed in 2015 increased the size of the Chamber of Deputies to 155 members and the Senate to 50, as of 2017. The law also requires political parties to have more women run for office.

Chile has a number of political parties that hold different ideas about how the country should be governed. At times, parties with similar ideas unite to form a coalition. The two

Chileans as young as twenty-one are eligible to run for the Chamber of Deputies. In 2013, Camila Vallejo won a seat when she was just twenty-five years old. But Vallejo was no stranger to politics. In the years before she was elected, she helped lead protests against Chile's educational system. Vallejo and thousands of other students wanted free education for all Chileans. They forced the country to look at how it could improve its schools. When Vallejo ran for the Chamber of Deputies, she walked through her entire district to talk to voters. She hoped her election meant Chile was ready to make changes in its government to help all Chileans and ensure greater economic equality.

leading coalitions are the New Majority, which includes socialists and Christian Democrats, and the more conservative Alianza (Alliance).

In addition to creating laws, members of the National Congress must approve international treaties before they take effect. The Chamber of Deputies can investigate whether the president or other officials have broken the law. If the deputies believe they have, the Senate acts as a jury to decide if the officials are innocent or guilty. The Senate also must approve certain officials appointed by the president, including some judges.

The Executive Branch

The executive branch carries out the laws of a country. The leader of Chile's executive branch is the president, who is elected every four years. If more than two candidates run and

The National Anthem

The music to Chile's national anthem—"Himno Nacional de Chile"—was composed by Ramón Carnicer and the words are by Eusebio Lillo. It was adopted in 1828.

Spanish lyrics

Puro, Chile, es tu cielo azulado;
Puras brisas te cruzan también.
Y tu campo de flores bordado
Es la copia feliz del Edén.
Majestuosa es la blanca montaña
Que te dio por baluarte el Señor
Que te dio por baluarte el Señor,
Y ese mar que tranquilo te baña
Te promete futuro esplendor
Y ese mar que tranquilo te baña
Te promete futuro esplendor.

Dulce Patria, recibe los votos
Con que Chile en tus aras juró:
Que o la tumba serás de los libres
O el asilo contra la opresión
Que o la tumba serás de los libres
O el asilo contra la opresión
Que o la tumba serás de los libres
O el asilo contra la opresión
O el asilo contra la opresión
O el asilo contra la opresión.

English translation

Pure, Chile, is your blue sky;
Pure breezes flow across you as well.
And your flower-embroidered field
Is a happy copy of Eden.
Majestic is the (white) snow-capped mountain
That was given as a bastion by the Lord
That was given as a bastion by the Lord,
And the sea that quietly washes your shores
Promises you future splendor
And the sea that quietly washes your shores
Promises you future splendor.

Sweet fatherland, accept the vows
That were given by Chile at your altars:
Either you be the tomb of the free
Or the refuge against oppression
Either you be the tomb of the free
Or the refuge against oppression
Either you be the tomb of the free
Or the refuge against oppression
Or the refuge against oppression
Or the refuge against oppression.

In 2006, Chileans elected their first female president, Michelle Bachelet. She became active in politics while studying medicine during the presidency of Salvador Allende. Like him, she is a socialist. Her father served in the Allende government and was arrested when Augusto Pinochet took power. He later died in prison. Michelle Bachelet was also arrested and was briefly held in prison. After her release, she lived overseas until 1979.

In 2000, Bachelet became minister of health. She also took an interest in military affairs and became minister of defense in 2002. During her first term as president, from 2006 to 2010, Bachelet stressed helping the poor, women, and the Mapuche. After leaving office, she led a United Nations organization that promoted the rights of women. When Bachelet ran for president again in 2013, she promised to make changes to the education system and call for a new constitution. She won the runoff easily.

nobody receives more than half the vote, the two candidates who received the most votes face each other in a special election called a runoff. Chile's president cannot serve two terms in a row, but can leave office and run again after four years.

Chile's president can propose laws. He or she also appoints cabinet members, who lead different departments and advise the president on important issues. The departments in the executive branch include national defense, finance, foreign affairs, justice, environment, and health. With the Senate's approval, Chile's president also appoints the comptroller general, who has a wide range of duties. This person examines

The bottom half of Chile's flag is red, which represents the blood shed during the fight for independence. Above it is a blue square with a white star. The blue stands for the sky, and the star symbolizes the power of government. Next to the square is a white stripe, which stands for the snow on the Andes. The flag was adopted in 1817.

The president's residence and offices are in La Moneda, which means "the coin." The building was originally a colonial mint, a place where coins are made.

how money is collected and spent at the national and local levels, making sure all laws are followed. The comptroller also examines presidential orders—called decrees—and new laws to see if they follow existing laws and the country's constitution. The president can overrule a comptroller general's decision to stop a decree from taking effect, but every cabinet minister must approve the president's action.

A Look at the Capital

Santiago, Chile's capital and largest city, was founded in 1541. A few buildings date back to the colonial era, such as the president's office building, called La Moneda. Construction on it began in 1784.

Today, Santiago has a population of about 5,128,041. It is an energetic city, lively and worldly. Santiago is the banking, industrial, political, and cultural capital of the country.

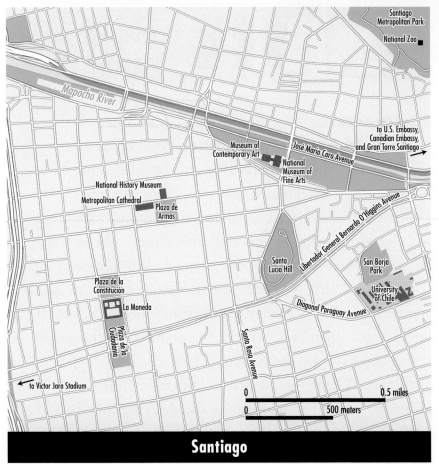

Santiago

Residents of the capital city live in thirty-two distinct neighborhoods. Some are marked by expensive buildings, while others have sprawling markets where handmade goods from across the country are sold.

A popular gathering spot is the Plaza de Armas, the heart of the city. Several important buildings line the plaza, including the National History Museum and the Metropolitan Cathedral. The city also has modern skyscrapers, including the Gran Torre Santiago. At almost 1,000 feet (305 m), it's the tallest building in South America.

The Chilean Supreme Court Building was constructed between 1905 and 1930.

Judicial Branch

The judicial branch hears two different kinds of court cases. Criminal cases involve the breaking of laws, while civil cases involve disputes between groups or people. At the lower level of the system are district courts that focus on certain areas of law, including criminal acts or family issues. Above these courts are sixteen courts of appeal, where justices review cases tried in lower courts. Cases heard in these courts can also be appealed to Chile's highest court, the Supreme Court. It has twenty-one members, who are appointed by the president and approved by the Senate. Chile also has a separate Constitutional Court that decides if laws follow the country's constitution. Special courts hear cases involving members of the military, and an elections court makes sure all elections are carried out fairly.

Regional and Local Governments

Chile is divided into fifteen regions. The president appoints officials called *intendentes* to run the regions. Most of the regions are divided into smaller areas, called provinces, which are headed by governors also chosen by the president. Within the provinces are municipalities—towns and cities—which are led by elected mayors. A mayor works with an elected council to run a municipality. Regional and local officials try to create jobs, protect the public's safety, and keep order. Unlike states in the United States, regions and provinces do not have their own legislative branches.

A woman in Santiago casts a ballot in a presidential election. Chileans must be at least eighteen years old to vote.

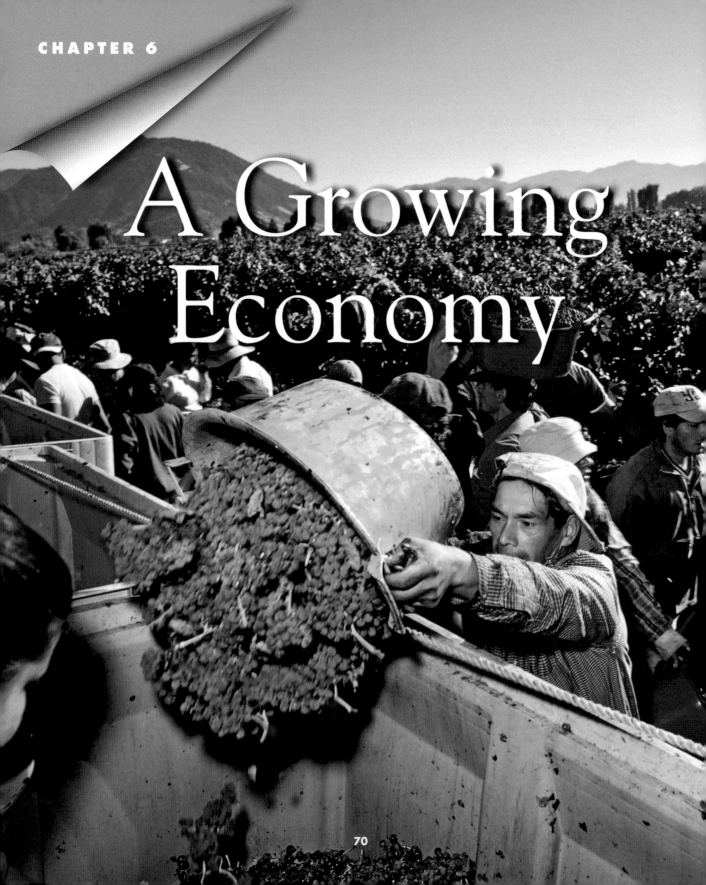

CHAPTER 6

A Growing Economy

CHILE HAS ONE OF THE STRONGEST ECONOMIES IN South America, an economy that is closely tied to the rest of the world. Chileans raise crops, catch fish, and mine resources that are sold around the globe. Factories also make items that are sold overseas. In 2013, Chile's exports, the goods it sold in other countries, totaled US$79.4 billion. Many of the exports went to China, the United States, and Japan. Chile also needs to buy goods from other countries. Its imports include cars, computers, and oil.

Opposite: **Workers harvest grapes at a vineyard in central Chile. About eight thousand farms in Chile produce grapes for wine.**

Copper Is King

Mining copper and other ores has long been Chile's major industry. Chile leads the world in copper production, and raw copper and copper products are the country's top exports. They were worth about US$40 billion in 2013. The area

A truck hauls rock from a huge copper mine in Chile.

around Antofagasta has the world's most productive copper mines. The country is thought to have enough copper in the ground to keep mining it for up to two hundred years.

Chile is also a world leader in mining molybdenum, an ore mixed with other metals to make them stronger. Other mines in the country produce iron ore, gold, sodium and potassium nitrate, zinc, silver, and coal.

Fields and Forests

In 2014, only about 3 percent of Chileans worked in agriculture, but they produced some of the country's most important

In the isolated salt flats of the Atacama Desert, flamingos share space with one of Chile's newest valuable resources—lithium. This light metal is used in many industries and is a key part of the rechargeable batteries found in many electronic devices.

To extract the metal, lithium salts are put in large ponds. The sun evaporates the water, leaving a highly concentrated form of lithium behind. Chile's northern region, along with neighboring Bolivia, contains the world's largest known supply of lithium. But a law passed in 1986 limited the number of companies that could mine it to two. Seeing the rising demand for lithium, in 2014 President Michelle Bachelet created a government commission to look at how to expand production. The commission created a government-owned company to start mining the metal.

goods. Chile is a major producer of grapes both for eating and for making wine. Chile's farms produce apples, pears, peaches, blueberries, cherries, avocados, onions, and asparagus. Other farm products include nuts, corn, oats, and beef. Since it is winter in North America and other parts of the world when it is summer in Chile, Chilean farmers grow a lot of the fresh produce sold during the winter in those northern regions.

Along with growing crops, Chileans also turn much of their fresh produce into processed foods. The processing includes drying, canning, and freezing. For example, some grapes are dried to make raisins, and fruits and vegetables are frozen. About half of the crops grown are turned into processed foods, and most of those are sold overseas.

Resources

Cereals and fruit	Ag	Silver	Li	Lithium
Livestock ranching	Au	Gold	Mo	Molybdenum
Seasonal grazing	C	Coal	N	Nitrates
Forests	Cu	Copper	Pb	Lead
Nonagricultural land	Fe	Iron Ore	Zn	Zinc

Workers stack firewood at a site in central Chile.

Trees cover a little more than 20 percent of Chile's land area, and products from trees play an important role in the economy. In 2013, the forestry industry provided jobs for more than one hundred thousand Chileans, and exports were worth more than US$5 billion. Radiata pine and eucalyptus trees are especially important to the industry, which is centered along the southern coast of the

Nuts for the World

Growing and drying nuts for export is an expanding part of Chile's farming industry. Most of the nuts are sold overseas. Nut exports were worth about US$25 million in 2002 but had grown to more than US$321 million in 2014. The major nuts produced are walnuts, hazelnuts, and almonds. Some grape farmers have switched to raising walnuts because they take less water to grow and fewer workers to harvest.

What Chile Grows, Makes, and Mines

AGRICULTURE (2012)

Grapes	32,000,000 metric tons
Milk	26,500,999 metric tons
Sugar beets	18,200,000 metric tons

MANUFACTURING (VALUE OF EXPORTS)

Wood products (2014)	US$5.4 billion
Processed foods (2013)	US$4.4 billion
Chemical products (2013)	US$3.2 billion

MINING (2013)

Iron ore	17,000,000 metric tons
Salt	6,500,000 metric tons
Copper	5,800,000 metric tons

country. Chile's forest products include lumber, wood chips, cellulose—which is used to make cardboard and paper—and finished wood products, such as door frames.

Fishing for Food

Chile's fishers have made the country one of the world's leading sources of seafood. Some fishers sail out of villages in small boats, while others work on much larger ships. Off Chile's Pacific coast, the Peru Current carries cold water northward from Antarctica. This current helps create perfect living conditions for a wide variety of fish. Warmer waters in the north also have a range of fish. Fishers catch sea bass, shellfish,

anchovies, and mackerel. They also raise a growing number of salmon, trout, and shellfish on fish farms. Most of the farmed fish is sent overseas, either frozen or in cans. All together, the value of wild and farmed fish produced in Chile in 2013 was more than US$7 billion.

Making Goods

Chile has more than seven thousand manufacturing companies. Most major industries are located in the central part of the country, near Santiago and Valparaíso. The products made in Chilean factories include textiles, plastics, iron, steel, cement, and machinery. Much of the machinery is used to process goods from Chile's mining, forestry, and farming industries.

Energy production for Chileans is one key industry. Oil is refined for use as gasoline. Some of the oil is also turned into chemicals. The country's rivers also help supply energy. Hydroelectric plants convert the energy in rushing water into electricity with the use of large blades called turbines. Electric companies wanted to build more dams for hydroelectric power on Patagonia's Baker and Pascua Rivers, but in 2014 the government turned them down. Leaders feared the dams might hurt the environment along the rivers.

Food processing is one of Chile's major manufacturing industries. Here, a worker stacks meat products at a plant in southern Chile.

Service Industries

The service sector of an economy includes government services, education, engineering, retail sales, insurance, health and

Eyes on the Skies

Chile is home to some of the world's most powerful telescopes. Building and running these telescopes provides jobs and helps Chile play an important role in studying space. In 2014 and 2015, construction began on two new telescopes. The European Extremely Large Telescope will feature a mirror 128 feet (39 m) wide, ten times larger than similar telescopes already in use. The Giant Magellan Telescope (right) will use several mirrors to locate distant objects in space. Both telescopes should begin operating in the early 2020s.

legal services, and communications, among others. The service sector makes up the largest share of Chile's economy. In 2015, it produced about 62 percent of the country's gross domestic product—the total of all goods and services produced.

Banking is a major service industry in Chile, which has one of the oldest banking systems in Latin America. In recent times, Chile has become a financial center for South America, thanks to its educated workers and laws that promote business and investing.

The government also promotes the making of computer software. In recent years, several U.S. companies have set up offices in Santiago to develop new software. The companies are attracted by the low cost of doing business there and the well-educated workforce. The government is also encouraging Chileans to start their own technology companies.

Tourism is another important part of the service economy. Several million foreigners come to Chile each year, and Chileans visit sites in their own country. Tourists take part in

outdoor sports, visit national parks, and explore museums. In 2014, about 250,000 Chileans worked in the tourist industry. Some worked in restaurants or hotels, while others worked as tour guides or in museums.

Tourists kayak near an iceberg in Patagonia.

Money Facts

The basic unit of currency in Chile is the Chilean peso. Chile issues coins worth 1, 5, 10, 50, 100, and 500 pesos and bills worth 1,000, 2,000, 5,000, 10,000, and 20,000 pesos. Chile's bills feature the faces of famous Chileans on the front. A new 1,000-peso note appeared in 2011 that depicts Captain Ignacio Carerra Pinto, who served in the army during the 1879 War of the Pacific. He was the grandson of José Miguel Carrera, one of the heroes of Chile's fight for independence from Spain. In 2016, US$1.00 equaled 727 Chilean pesos.

A Growing Economy **79**

CHAPTER 7

The People
of Chile

THE FIRST SETTLERS OF CHILE WERE THE ANCESTORS of today's Mapuche and other indigenous peoples. Thousands of years later, indigenous people watched outsiders come to their land. The newcomers included Incas, Spaniards and other Europeans, and people from the Middle East. Also, Africans were kidnapped and taken to Peru, where they were forced into slavery.

The people of different ethnic groups sometimes married, and their children became mestizos, people with a mixed ethnic background. While Spain made the most lasting impact on Chile, Chileans today have blended arts, foods, and ideas from many parts of the world. That variety adds to the vibrant cultural life Chileans enjoy.

Opposite: **Chileans play chess on the street in Santiago.**

Ethnic Chile	
White and nonindigenous	88.9%
Mapuche	9.1%
Aymara	0.7%
Other indigenous groups	1.0%
Unspecified	0.3%

Persons per square mile		Persons per square kilometer
more than 130		more than 50
27–130		11–50
14–26		6–10
3–13		1–5
fewer than 3		fewer than 1

The Lasting Spanish Influence

Spaniards traveling through Chile hear many things that might remind them of home. They hear people speaking Spanish, though some words are pronounced slightly differently, and some words have a different meaning. The Mapuche and immigrants have shaped *castellano*—the version of Spanish spoken in Chile. The word refers to Castile, a region of Spain.

Many of the original Spanish settlers were poor and borrowed money to move to Chile. Some of the settlers were merchants, hoping to make money from trade. The elite that ruled the country came mostly from Castile and from the Basque Country, a region along the Pyrenees Mountains in Spain and France.

In recent years, new Spanish-speaking residents have arrived in Chile from neighboring countries in South America. Most of these new-

The Basque of Chile

The Basque people speak their own language that is not related to any other language from Europe. Some of the first government officials in colonial Chile were Basque. Other Basques excelled in business. Today, many of Chile's wealthiest families trace their roots to the Basque Country. In the eighteenth century, wealthy Basques created an organization to help Basque immigrants settling in Chile. More Basques arrived in Chile during the 1930s, when a civil war in Spain forced many of them to flee their home country and Chile welcomed them. Today, the Basque in Chile have their own social groups to promote their ethnic identity.

comers are from Peru and settle in and around Santiago. Many work in the homes of wealthier Chileans. A sizable number of immigrants also come from Argentina and Bolivia. Some Spaniards still arrive, too.

A Peruvian immigrant in Santiago works restoring furniture. More than 350,000 people have moved to Chile in recent years, looking for better economic opportunities than they could find in their home countries.

Get It? Chilean Expressions

Chileans have expressions not used in other Spanish-speaking lands. These are sometimes called Chilenismos. Here are a few:

Chilenismos	Literal translation	Meaning
¿Cachai?	Catch?	Get it/understand?
Tiene cueva	He has a cave	He is lucky
Dejar la escoba	To leave a broom	To make a mess
Buena onda	A good wave (sea)	Great stuff, cool
No estar ni ahi	I am not even there	I don't care
Eres pesado	You are heavy	You are being a nuisance

Population of Major Cities (2014 est.)

Santiago	5,128,041
Puente Alto	802,109
Antofagasta	390,832
San Bernardo	316,094
Viña del Mar	288,329
Temuco	264,642

Other Immigrants

During the nineteenth century, some newcomers, including many Germans, arrived in Chile from Europe. Some of the Germans founded the town of Puerto Montt, and many of them opened businesses in Valdivia. German names are still seen in these areas, and some German-Chileans still cook German-style foods. Italians and Croatians also moved to Chile, as did Chinese people. Several thousand Chinese still immigrate to Chile each year.

Starting in the early twentieth century, Arab-speaking people from the Middle East began to arrive. Most came from Lebanon and Syria and belonged to Christian churches. During this time, their native lands were controlled by the Turks, who were Muslims and sometimes mistreated the local Christians. Many of the Arabs settled in the town of La Calera, in the Valle Central.

In recent years, Chile has accepted about two thousand

people each year who were fleeing war or other trouble in their homelands. They have come from such nations as Afghanistan, Rwanda, Iraq, and Haiti.

Many Chilean citizens have moved abroad, seeking better jobs than they can find at home. Argentina has the largest

The city of Puerto Varas, in south-central Chile, is known for its German-style architecture. Traditional German foods are also popular in the city.

What's in a Name?

Chileans, like people in other Spanish-speaking lands, often have two last names. First is the father's family name and second is the mother's family name. In practice, only the father's last name is commonly used for the children's last name. The full name of Chile's president is Michelle Bachelet Jeria, but she is usually called Michelle Bachelet. Like most Chilean women, she kept her own name when she married.

Three generations of a Mapuche family in southern Chile. The average family in Chile has two children.

Chilean community outside the country, with more than four hundred thousand people.

Indigenous Chileans

As of 2012, Chile had about 1.7 million people who said they have indigenous roots. The Mapuche make up almost 90 percent of that number. Today many live in the Santiago region or in the city of Temuco, but some remain on Mapuche lands in the south. They continue to fight legal battles to regain more of the land they lost to Chilean settlers in the region. In 2014, President Michelle Bachelet offered them some hope when she called for policies that would return more land to the Mapuche.

The next-largest indigenous group is the Aymara, with a population of about 119,000. Most Aymara live in the northern Andes and altiplano, near the borders with Bolivia and Peru. Larger numbers of Aymara live in Bolivia and Peru. Other indigenous peoples of Chile include the Quechua, Likan Antai, Colla, Diaguita, Kaweskar, and Yamana.

Easter Island is the home of the Rapa Nui. They trace their roots to Polynesians, the indigenous people of islands scattered around the South Pacific. As many as twelve thousand Rapa Nui once lived on the island. When Europeans arrived,

Speak Like a Mapuche

The Mapuche language is called Mapudungun. It uses six vowel sounds:

a is similar to the a in "man"

e is similar to the e in "end"

i is similar to the i in "pin"

o is similar to the o in "cold"

u is similar to the oo in "moon"

the sixth vowel ï sounds like a u but with the lips placed as if saying e

Here are some words in Mapudungun:

kiñe	one
epu	two
küla	three
nuke	mother
chaw	father

Some Mapuche words are used throughout Chile. The name for the national flower, the copihue, is a Mapuche word, as are the names of many geographic sites.

however, they brought diseases that wiped out many of the local people. The native people had not been exposed to these diseases before, so their bodies did not have immunities to them and could not fight off the illnesses. The Europeans also enslaved some of the Rapa Nui. Today, Chile is home to about eight thousand Rapa Nui. Some live on Easter Island, and some live on the mainland.

A Rapu Nui couple from Easter Island. Nearly six thousand people live on Easter Island today.

Afro-Chileans

A small number of Chileans trace their roots to Africa. Some Africans came with the Spanish conquistadores. Both enslaved and free Africans lived in colonial Chile. African slaves also lived in Arica, Peru, a region that became part of Chile after the War of the Pacific ended in 1884. Arica remains the center of African-Chilean culture. The Chilean census has never had a category for people of African descent, but by some estimates there are about eight thousand Afro-Chileans. In 2013, the government began its first study of the Afro-Chilean population in and around Arica. Several groups have formed the Afro-Chilean Alliance, bringing attention to Afro-Chileans and their fight to be recognized as a distinct ethnic group.

Women dance in a parade celebrating Afro-Chilean heritage.

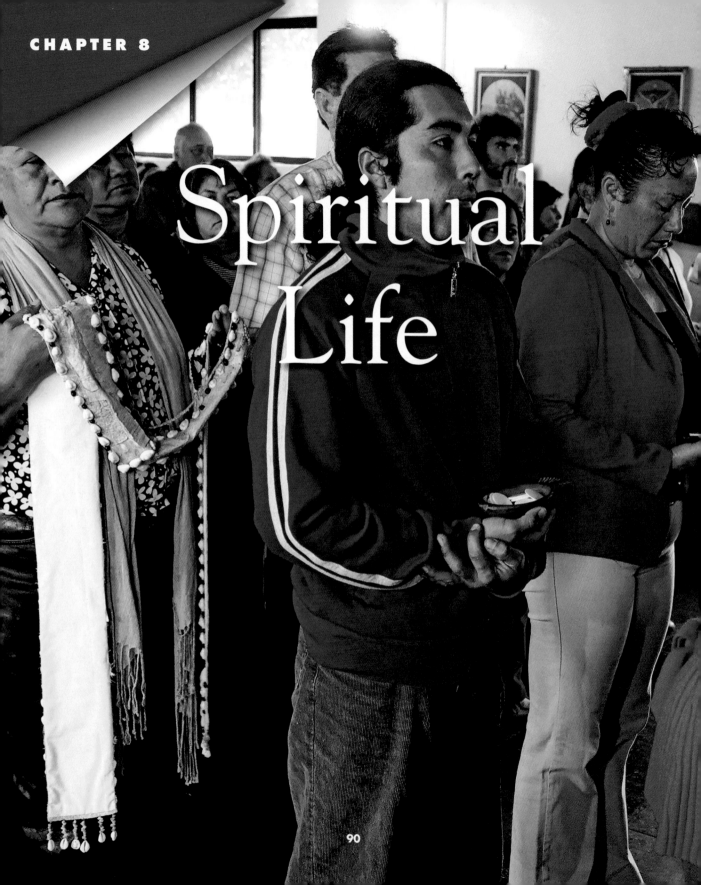

CHAPTER 8

Spiritual Life

WHEN SPAIN COLONIZED CHILE, IT WAS NOT only seeking wealth. King Charles V also wanted to spread Roman Catholicism, his country's religion, across South America. Traveling with the conquistadores were Roman Catholic priests who tried to teach Roman Catholic beliefs to the indigenous people of Chile. Some of the Aymara and Mapuche accepted the new faith, but others did not. Some indigenous people mixed their traditional beliefs with Catholicism.

Over the centuries, immigrants from other lands brought their religions to Chile. Today, the country has people who follow Judaism, Islam, Buddhism, and a variety of Protestant beliefs. And some Mapuche and other indigenous people still follow their traditional beliefs. The Chilean constitution guarantees people the right to worship as they choose. The Roman Catholic Church, however, remains the largest and most powerful church in the nation.

Opposite: **Catholic Chileans attend mass in a church on Easter Island.**

Santiago's Metropolitan Cathedral lies in the heart of the Plaza de Armas. The grand building dates to the 1700s.

Religion in Chile	
Roman Catholic	67%
Protestant	16%
Jehovah's Witness	1%
Other	3%
None	12%
Not specified	1%

The Catholic Church

The first Catholic services in Santiago were held in a simple hut that collapsed after a few years. Priests then constructed churches that lasted, with the help of wealthy Chileans who donated land and money. The priests and monks in Chile used some of this wealth to build and run schools, hospitals, and orphanages.

After Chile gained independence, some of its leaders tried to weaken the power of the Roman Catholic Church. These leaders did not want the church to dictate laws or have sole control over marriage. Some Chileans, however, resisted the effort to weaken the church's influence. The struggle between devout Catholics and those who opposed the church's influence continued. For example, divorce is against Catholic teachings, and Chile did not allow divorce until 2004.

Saints play an important role in the Roman Catholic faith. The church recognizes saints for their good deeds and strong belief in Catholic teachings. Some Catholics pray to saints when they face problems in their lives. The first Chilean named a saint was Juana Fernández y Solar. Born in 1900, she showed a deep interest in her faith while still a young girl. She wrote many letters that reflected her love of Jesus Christ. At age nineteen, she became a nun and took the name Teresa. She died shortly after, but she had already shown a strong commitment to Catholicism. In 1993, she became the first saint from Chile and she is known today as St. Teresa of the Andes.

At times Catholic leaders have spoken out against injustice. During and after General Augusto Pinochet's rule, the church tried to help victims of government torture. In recent years, Chile's Catholic officials have supported the rights of the Mapuche.

Children in Catholic families are baptized soon after they are born and are expected to go through other important Catholic rites. These include first communion, confirmation, and marriage in a Catholic church. Across the country, festivals and parades mark the days set aside for the saints. In December, the northern town of Andacollo has a festi-

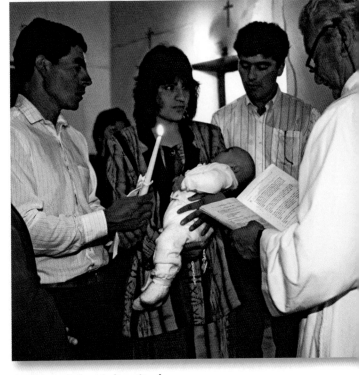

A Chilean infant is baptized.

val that honors a statue of the Virgin Mary that is said to answer people's prayers. For four days, people wear costumes and dance in the streets. The festival attracts up to one hundred thousand people from all over Chile.

Pilgrims carry a statue of the Virgin Mary through the streets of Andacollo. Each December, thousands of people arrive in the town to take part in the festival honoring the statue.

Other Christian Faiths

Under Spanish rule, only Catholics could live in Chile. With independence, though, the new government welcomed Protestants who could help Chile's economy grow. Many English merchants belonged to the Anglican Church, which is known as

the Episcopal Church in the United States. The German settlers who came in the nineteenth century were typically Lutherans.

Today, Chile's Protestants also include Methodists and Presbyterians. Many Protestants in the country call themselves Pentecostal. In Pentecostal churches, the services are filled with emotion and music, and some members believe that their Christian faith can cure the sick. Chile's Methodist Pentecostal Church has more than eight hundred thousand members.

Today, Chile also has a growing number of Mormons, people who belong to the Church of Jesus Christ of Latter-day Saints. About five hundred thousand people belong to this church. Chile also has a notable number of Jehovah's Witnesses.

Protestants sing during a church service in Santiago. The number of evangelical Protestants in Chile is growing.

A mosque, or Muslim house of worship, sits atop a hill in Coquimbo.

Non-Christian Faiths

The first Spaniards to reach Chile included some Jews known as *conversos*. The Spanish government had outlawed their faith, so they converted to Roman Catholicism. Some, though, still practiced Judaism in secret. Jews could openly practice their religion after Chile gained its independence. Some Jewish immigrants from Europe settled in the country during the nineteenth century. Thousands more came during the 1930s, when Germany passed laws denying its Jews legal rights. Today, Chile has a Jewish population of about eighteen thousand.

Chile has just a small number of Muslims, followers of Islam. Many are immigrants from the Middle East, but some Chileans have converted to Islam. The country's first mosque, where Muslim religious services are held, opened in Santiago in 1995. The first Muslim cemetery opened in 2010. Other small, non-Christian populations in Chile include Buddhists and Baha'is.

Mapuche Beliefs

While many indigenous people adopted the Catholic faith, some still follow their traditional religions. The Mapuche people's religion teaches that the world is filled with positive and negative forces. The Mapuche also believe that mounds they built long ago are living things filled with the spirits of the dead. They honor the dead by placing wooden statues called *chemamulles* on the mounds. The most important religious figures for the Mapuche are called *machi*. Both men and women can be

Traditionally, wooden statues called chemamulles were part of the funeral ceremony for Mapuche people. A chemamull was placed beside the body while members of the community described the deceased person's achievements in life. Then, once the body was buried, the chemamull marked the gravesite.

machi. They lead religious ceremonies and are thought to make contact with spirits that most people cannot hear or see.

One of the most important tasks machi perform is healing the sick. They might look at a patient's palm or feel his or her pulse. Treatments usually rely on herbs that the Mapuche have used as medicine for centuries. Once only Mapuche came to the machi with their health problems. Today, though, anyone in Santiago can see the machi, who work out of several health clinics there. The Mapuche view of medicine is based partly on the idea that people become ill when their inner spirit is suffering in some way. Prayer is often part of the treatment.

A Mapuche machi, or shaman, in southern Chile. Most machi are women.

Life on Chiloé

Before the Spanish came to Chile, some Mapuche settled on the island of Chiloé. They followed the island's first settlers, the Chonos. Together, the people of Chiloé created stories that are known today across Chile. One story tells how the island was created after the battle between two giant sea serpents. Different gods and goddesses were said to live nearby, including the beautiful goddess Pincoya. She lived in the seas and provided fish for humans to eat. Pincoya was also said to help sailors who fell overboard, though others said she trapped men attracted by her good looks. The people of Chiloé also believed a ghost ship called Caleuche carried away people who died at sea.

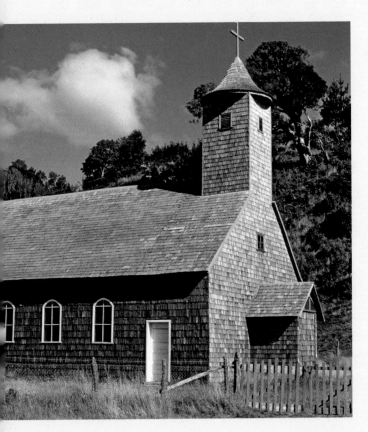

In time, the residents of the island converted to Christianity, and they began to build small, wooden chapels along the coast. The people did not have nails, so they used wooden pegs to hold the chapels together. Today, sixteen of the wooden chapels are listed on the United Nations Educational, Scientific and Cultural Organization's (UNESCO) list of World Heritage sites. The honor recognizes the chapels' unique wooden architecture, a blend of indigenous and Spanish culture.

CHAPTER 9

Arts and Entertainment

CHILE HAS A LONG ARTISTIC TRADITION. BEFORE the Spanish arrived, indigenous people made handsome and useful goods, such as pots and cloth. The Mapuche made beautiful copper goods. They later used those skills to make silver items ranging from belts and pins to horse stirrups. Beautifully carved wooden masks and altars were used during religious ceremonies.

Over the centuries, music and dance have also been an important part of Mapuche creativity. Their musical instruments include a wooden drum called a *kultrun*, a long bamboo trumpet called a *trutruka*, and stone flutes. Machi use kultruns during religious rites.

Opposite: **Mapuche jewelry often includes long plates of metal.**

Gabriela Mistral was the first Spanish-speaking poet and the first Latin American woman to receive the Nobel Prize in Literature.

The Value of Writing

Alonso de Ercilla was a sixteenth-century Spanish soldier who fought against the Mapuche. He was also a poet and wrote Chile's first great literary work, *La Araucana*. The poem describes the conflict between the Spanish and the Mapuche and honors the Indians for their bravery. Thanks to *La Araucana*, many future Chileans also came to admire the Mapuche.

Poetry emerged as one of modern Chile's great arts during the twentieth century. Poets formed societies so they could inspire one another. The country's first great poets included

Vicente Huidobro and Gabriela Mistral. Huidobro wrote experimental poems that incorporated random words and letters. Mistral produced very different kinds of poems, writing about experiences from her life. She won the 1945 Nobel Prize in Literature, the world's highest literary honor.

Mistral was also a teacher. She taught Pablo Neruda, who became another of Chile's great poets, writing about politics, love, and the lives of average Chileans. In 1971, Neruda also won a Nobel Prize.

Chile has produced novelists as well. José Donoso began publishing during the 1950s and became one of the greatest modern writers in South America. Donoso's novels, including *The Obscene Bird of Night* and *The Garden Next Door*, are sometimes described as magical realism. They mix seemingly

Pablo Neruda's Death

Like many Chilean artists of the time, Pablo Neruda supported Salvador Allende and opposed the takeover of the government by General Augusto Pinochet. In September 1973, Neruda hoped to leave the country and stir up public opinion against the junta. But before he could leave, he died at a Santiago hospital. At the time, the government claimed he died of cancer. Many people suspected, however, that he may have been murdered, and that the murderer probably had ties to Pinochet. In 2015, the government admitted that there was a chance that Neruda did not die of natural causes. The government's announcement convinced many Chileans that their greatest poet was killed for his political beliefs.

Roberto Bolaño was both a poet and a novelist.

impossible situations into the lives of regular people, often with plenty of humor. Another Chilean novelist, Roberto Bolaño, produced moody, intense works that won great praise. These include *The Savage Detectives* and *2666*.

A Chilean Author in America

Isabel Allende, a niece of Salvador Allende, began her writing career as a journalist in Chile. She fled the country when the military took control. Allende started writing novels while living in Venezuela. Her first book, *The House of the Spirits*, won wide praise. She often uses magical realism to tell her stories, and she draws on Chilean history and culture for some of her work. Her 2003 book *My Invented Country* explores her own experiences in her homeland.

Allende became a U.S. citizen in 1993, and in 2014 U.S. president Barack Obama awarded her the Presidential Medal of Freedom, the highest honor a U.S. citizen can receive.

A Musical Land

The Spanish brought guitars to Chile, where the indigenous people played many types of drums and pipes. Both Spanish and indigenous musical traditions survive in Chile, and the country has also been influenced by popular music from other parts of the world.

Some folk instruments still played today are the *zampoña*, the *charango*, and the *wada*. The zampoña is a kind of panpipe, which has a series of tubes with one end open and one closed. The tubes of various lengths are tied together from shortest to

A musician in Santiago plays a zampoña.

longest. Blowing into the tubes creates notes. The wada is a dried pumpkin filled with seeds or stones. When a musician shakes the wada, the seeds bounce around, creating a rhythmic sound.

After the Spanish arrived, folk musicians called *payadores* became common in Chile. A payador traveled from town to town with a guitar, making up songs on the spot. Later, musicians sometimes formed clubs, called *peñas*, where people gathered to play and hear folk music.

Chilean folk music often includes guitars.

One of the best-known Chilean musicians outside the country is Ana Tijoux. Her parents were arrested when General Augusto Pinochet came to power. They later moved to France, where Tijoux was born. She moved to Chile after democracy was restored and joined the hip-hop group Mazika. On her own, she recorded a song that was used on the U.S. TV show *Breaking Bad*. Tijoux has been nominated for several Grammy Awards, the highest honor in the music business. Like many Chilean musicians since the 1960s, Tijoux writes songs about politics and social issues, such as the inequality many women face and the power the wealthy have over governments.

Starting in the 1960s, Chile's tradition of folk music inspired new singers and songwriters. They wrote songs that used familiar melodies but added words that described the struggles of Chile's poor and working class. This new folk music was called *nueva canción Chilena*, "new Chilean song." Violeta Parra was called the mother of this form of music. She educated young Chileans about their country's musical traditions. Her grandson, Angel, joined the rock group Los Tres, which has won fans around the world. Newer musical acts that have won international attention include the rock band Astro, and singer-songwriter Javiera Mena, who combines electronic and pop music to make dance music.

Dancers never touch while performing the cueca. The dance is often performed on national holidays in Chile.

A Land of Dance

Dancing is a major part of Chile's traditional culture. Different dances are favored in different parts of the country. In the north, several traditional dances feature a large circle, with two or more dancers entering the middle of it. In the central part of Chile, one popular dance is the *sombrerito*, or little hat. At one point, the dancers make a figure 8 as they move around a hat placed on the ground. The Mapuche created the *choique purun*, in which the dancers imitate the movements of the rhea.

The *cueca*, the official dance of Chile, is thought to have roots in either West Africa or Spain. In this dance, men dress like *huasos*, the cowboys of Chile, and women wear colorful dresses. In poorer communities, the dancers often wear simpler clothes and go barefoot. The cueca is said to copy the actions of a rooster trying to attract a female chicken. A man selects the woman he finds the prettiest, and the two hold on to a handkerchief. The man pulls on the cloth to bring the woman closer to him, and soon both dancers are stomping their feet. The dancers are surrounded by a circle of people who clap along. Slightly different versions of the cueca appear in different parts of the country.

Visual Arts

Chile has produced a number of talented painters and sculptors. Perhaps Chile's best-known painter is Roberto Matta, who, starting in the 1930s, created swirling, fantastical paintings. In more recent years, Arturo Duclos has worked with both paint and objects to present his view of the world. In

Art Underground

Easter Island is known for its immense stone figures that sit along the shore on part of the island. Called *moai*, they were carved by the Rapa Nui about eight hundred years ago. The average moai is 13 feet (4 m) tall and weighs 14 tons (12.7 metric tons). Many of the statues also have designs carved into them. In recent years, scientists have dug away the dirt around some of the moai to reveal they have bodies that had been buried over time. All moai have bodies, but many of the well-known photos of the Easter Island statues show ones that have only their heads and shoulders above the earth's surface. The scientists' work reveals the true size of many of the moai. The largest of the ones recently uncovered stand 30 feet (9 m) tall.

several pieces, he used human bones to create shapes and images, such as the Chilean flag. Gonzalo Cienfuegos often paints human figures in scenes from everyday life.

Chile also has a tradition of folk art. Murals—large, colorful paintings on buildings and walls—can be seen on many city streets. Valparaíso is especially known for these murals, and artists from all over the world travel to Valparaíso to paint them. Traditional crafts now considered folk art include basket

Students began painting murals on walls in Valparaíso in the late 1960s. Today, many of the city's brightly painted walls boast art.

weaving and pottery making. Pomaire, outside of Santiago, is famous for its potters. Artists in Chile also create small carvings and jewelry out of lapis lazuli, a blue stone.

The hills around Pomaire are filled with clay. As a result, the city became a center for Chilean pottery.

On Screen

Chilean filmmakers have worked both at home and abroad to create well-received movies. Alejandro Jodorowsky has made several films that have won praise from critics. His 2013 work *The Dance of Reality* examined his life growing up in northern Chile during the 1930s. Other Chilean filmmakers have won international honors. Andrés Wood won a prize at a U.S. film festival in 2012 for *Violeta Went to Heaven*. Pablo Larraín's *No* was nominated for an Oscar in 2013. The film looked at how opponents of Augusto Pinochet won the vote that forced him to leave office. In 2016, Larraín released a film about Pablo Neruda.

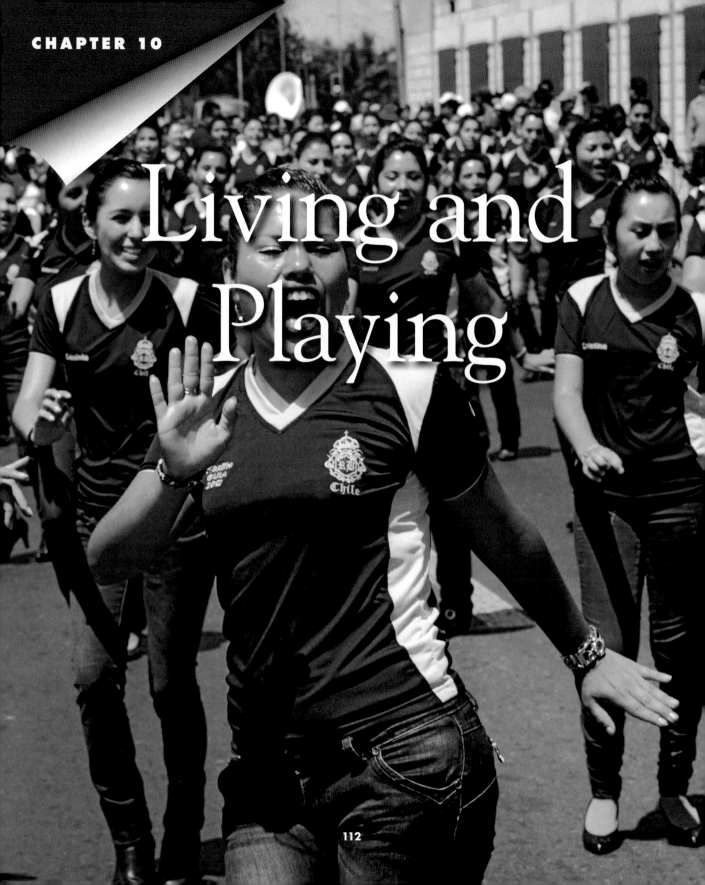

CHAPTER 10

Living and Playing

FOR MIGUEL LEIVA REYES, MANY THINGS STAND OUT about growing up in Chile. Though now a young adult, he has fond memories of his childhood, the foods he ate, and the games he played. At barbecues, he and other Chileans put *pebre* on their food, a sauce made with chilies, tomatoes, garlic, and onion. He also enjoyed the Chilean "hot dogs" called *completos*, made with sausage and topped with such things as avocado, tomatoes, and sauerkraut. During the national holidays in September, he and friends flew *volantínes*, or kites, and other days they played with *trompos*, wooden tops that are spun with a string. And he knows that for foreigners, even if they speak Spanish, Chileans are not always easy to talk to. He said, "We generally speak very fast, even mumbling sometimes, which can be very hard to understand [for] other Spanish speakers who are not used to it."

Opposite: **Women dance in the Andean Carnival parade in Pedro Montt.**

Rich, Poor, and in Between

Every Chilean's experiences are unique, of course. But Miguel's childhood and teen years were not unusual. Miguel and his family would be considered middle class. They have plenty of food and can afford cars, vacations, and video games, but they are not rich. Chile has the largest middle class in South America, with just over half the population falling into that class.

Most Chileans, regardless of their wealth, live in cities or other urban areas. Almost 90 percent of the people live in

A family enjoys ice cream on a stroll through Valparaíso.

Shacks spread out along a beach in northern Chile.

cities, with 40 percent of the population living in and around Santiago. In rural areas, some people still have trouble getting clean water, but on the whole Chile has made great gains in ending poverty. While 39 percent of the population lived in poverty in 1990, just 14 percent did in 2013.

Despite reducing the number of poor people, Chile still has a large gap in income between its wealthiest citizens and its poorest. A 2014 report showed that just nine Chilean families were worth about US$42 billion. They controlled 15 percent of the country's gross domestic product. The rich live in large homes, sometimes with guarded gates. The poorest people live in wooden shacks in the cities. In the countryside, some Mapuche live in houses topped with straw roofs, just as their ancestors did centuries ago.

Houses on the Move

For most people, moving means packing up what they own and taking it to their new home. On the island of Chiloé, however, some people move their home itself. Friends and neighbors help with the move, which is called a *minga*. The typical small houses found on the island are put on wooden rollers, which are pulled by oxen to their new location. Meanwhile, as that work goes on, women prepare a feast that everyone will enjoy when the move is done.

Work and School

For many middle-class Chileans, their day begins with a simple meal of buttered bread or cereal along with coffee or tea, and then it's off to work or school. Many families, not just the rich, have nannies or housekeepers to help take care of the children and the house. During the school year, parents bring their children to classes, which start around 8:00 a.m. The parents then head to their offices, and it's not uncommon for them to work past 6:00 p.m.

Along with working hard, Chileans value education. Almost 98 percent of the population can read and write. Children start school at age six and remain in school until they are seventeen. A growing number of young children attend preschool. Chile has a mixture of public schools that are run by local governments, schools for which parents pay some of the expenses, and completely private schools. In high school, students can take courses that will either prepare them for college or help them find jobs if they don't plan on going to college. As of 2013, 88 percent of Chileans between the ages of twenty-five and thirty-four had graduated from high school.

The number of Chileans who continue their education after high school is just over 50 percent. Chile's best universities are located in the major cities. Santiago is home to the country's oldest college, the University of Chile, which was founded in 1842. The capital is also home to the Pontifical Catholic University of Chile.

Chilean schoolchildren in Patagonia. Students at all schools in Chile wear uniforms.

Chileans have a variety of choices on how to get to school or work. Santiago has a modern subway system, called the Metro, and trains bring people into the city from the suburbs. The capital also has buses, and buses run within and between most cities. A special kind of bus is the *colectivo*. It runs on a set route, but will pick up and let off passengers wherever they want, like a taxi. In the countryside, people are more likely to use bikes and motorcycles to get around. In some remote areas, the roads are still unpaved, and cars are rare.

Many people in Chilean towns use bicycles to get around.

Time to Relax

On the weekends, Chileans enjoy getting together with family and friends. A typical welcome for a guest is the *abrazo*. Two people shake hands and hug, and a kiss is included for women and family members. In more formal settings, especially for men, a handshake is the usual greeting.

On any day, whether weekday or weekend, the main meal occurs at lunch and can last for several hours. Some businesses shut down during this time. In late afternoon, Chileans usually break for tea and snacks, a light meal sometimes called *once*. They then have their last meal of the day around 9:00 p.m. Adults might not go to bed until midnight.

To Chileans, fine food and drink are an important part of life, and meals are a relaxing time filled with good talk. Chilean wines are among the best in the world, and *pisco*, the national drink, is also made from grapes. Along the coast, people eat a variety of seafood. Inland, people are more likely to eat meat. Some favorite foods include *porotos con mazamorra*, which is white beans with corn, and *cazuela*, a soup with beef or chicken and potatoes, pumpkin, and corn. Chileans enjoy a variety of sandwiches. One of them is the *chacarero*, which has steak covered with tomatoes, boiled green beans, and green pepper. On Chiloé and in some areas in the south, people eat a stew called *curanto*. It features different kinds of meat, shellfish, and potatoes. The traditional way to prepare it is to dig a hole in the ground, fill it with hot rocks, and steam the food on the rocks.

It takes about an hour to cook curanto in the traditional way, on hot rocks.

A Warm and Tasty Sandwich

Chileans enjoy a delicious sandwich called the Barros Luco. It is named for a former president, Ramón Barros Luco. Some people compare it to the Philly cheesesteak sandwich found in the United States. Have an adult help you with this recipe.

Ingredients

1 sirloin steak
4 slices Monterey Jack cheese
4 rolls, sliced

Directions

Cook the steak in a pan and then slice it thinly. Put a slice of cheese on the inside top of each roll and broil them until the cheese starts to melt. Place the sliced meat on the bottom half of the rolls, and put the two halves of the roll together. Enjoy!

Alfajores are popular treats throughout South America.

A popular breakfast treat is *manjar*. Chileans take an unopened can of sweetened condensed milk and set it in boiling water for several hours. The cooking produces a thick, rich spread that can be smeared over bread. It's also a favorite afternoon snack for students after school. The heated, thickened milk is also used to make a dessert called *alfajor*. The manjar goes between layers of butter or sugar cookies, and the whole thing is covered with powdered sugar.

During warmer months, Chileans head outdoors for *asados*. Like barbecues in the United States, these special meals feature meat that has been roasted over hot coals or fire. Steak or a roast is usually the main course, and larger cuts of meat are often cooked on a stick over the fire. In Patagonia, whole goats or lambs are sometimes cooked this way, and diners then carve off pieces. When colder weather comes, some Chileans warm themselves with *pantrucas*. This soup has strips of dough that cook in a meat or vegetable broth.

Sports and Recreation

Chileans take part in a variety of sports for exercise and for fun. The favorite sport is soccer, which is played by both boys and girls. Chile's national men's soccer team is known as La Roja—"the red"—and the players wear red jerseys. La Roja has often appeared in the World Cup, soccer's most important event. Chile's top male players also play for professional teams around the world. One of the best was Iván "Bam Bam" Zamorano, who earned his nickname for his hard kicks. Chile also has its own professional soccer league.

Although not as popular as soccer, basketball is also played professionally in Chile. The country has a major professional league and attracts some players from the United States. Another popular sport in Chile is rodeo, one of Chile's national sports. In 2015, more than five hundred rodeos were held across the country. Riders earn points based on how well they can rope cows in a ring. Chileans also enjoy watching and playing tennis.

Rising Star

In recent years, Alexis Sánchez has taken Bam Bam Zamorano's place as Chile's top soccer player. Sometimes known simply as Alexis, he played his first international soccer match when he was just seventeen. Since then, he has played for Chile's national team and for several European teams. In 2014, he joined Arsenal, a team in England's top professional league. Alexis is a striker—a player expected to score goals. In his first year with Arsenal, he scored sixteen goals during the regular season.

Keeping Old Games Alive

While children in Chile love to play video games on their computers or phones, some still take part in traditional activities such as flying kites and spinning tops. Another old favorite game is *emboque*, the Chilean version of the cup-and-ball game. The emboque is a wooden bell-shaped top with a wooden stick attached by a string. The bottom of the bell has a narrow hole just big enough for the stick to enter. A player holds one end of the stick, tosses the bell into the air, and tries to catch the open end of the bell on the other end of the stick. The player who can catch the bell on the stick the most times in a row wins.

While not many people in Chile are gymnasts, the country has embraced Tomás González as one of its top international athletes. The gymnast won a gold medal at the 2012 World Cup and was the first Chilean gymnast to appear in the Olympics.

A Mapuche game called *palin* has been gaining popularity in recent years. Indigenous people were playing the sport, which is like field hockey, before the Spanish explorers arrived.

Chile's geography gives the residents easy access to both summer and winter sports. Chileans enjoy skiing and snowboarding in the Andes. They can also sail and swim in both the Pacific and the country's many lakes. Surfing, windsurfing, rafting, and kayaking are other popular water sports. Chileans also enjoy mountain biking and hiking. Starting in 2003, the government began building the Sendero de Chile, or Chilean Trail. When it is done, the trail will stretch more than 5,000 miles (8,000 km), running the length of the country.

Special Occasions

Festivals and holidays let Chileans take a break from their busy lives. In September, the whole country celebrates the *Fiestas Patrias*, or national holidays. September 18 and 19 are, respectively, Independence Day and Armed Forces Day. The celebration sometimes starts a few days before, with parades and dances. On Independence Day, people meet in parks to

Chilean rodeo is very different from American rodeo. In Chilean rodeo, two riders work together to pin a cow against the wall of the arena.

A Chilean Wedding

Many weddings in Chile take place in a Catholic church. Unlike most North American weddings, a Chilean wedding party does not always include a best man or maid of honor. Instead, the couples' parents join them at the altar. Also, the bride and groom give each other wedding rings when they become engaged. They wear the rings on their right hands until the wedding ceremony, when they switch the rings to the left hands. At the wedding reception, before the dancing begins, the bride and groom hand out hats, masks, necklaces, and other fun items for the guests to wear.

Children bike through Maipú, near Santiago, as part of the Cuasimodo festival.

eat delicious foods and dance the cueca. The next day, they honor the Chilean military with more parades—and more eating. The festivities may also include rodeos and games. Another big holiday is New Year's Day, which features huge fireworks displays in Santiago, Valparaíso, and other cities.

National Holidays and Festivals

New Year's Day	January 1
Easter Week	March/April
Labor Day	May 1
Navy Day	May 21
Corpus Christi	May/June
Day of San Pedro	June 29
Feast of Our Lady of Mount Carmel	July 16
Assumption	August 15
Independence Day	September 18
Armed Forces Day	September 19
Columbus Day	October 12
Reformation Day	October 29
All Saints' Day	November 1
Feast of the Immaculate Conception	December 8
Christmas	December 25

As a largely Roman Catholic country, Chileans celebrate several important religious holidays. Christmas and Easter are the two major ones. On Christmas Eve, many people go to church at midnight, and then come home to open presents. The next day is filled with food, usually an asado, since the holiday comes during the Chilean summer. Easter in Chile includes the Cuasimodo festival, a tradition that dates back to colonial times. The Sunday after Easter, huasos, priests, and local officials in towns around Santiago visit people too old or too sick to attend mass. Several thousand people join them as they make their rounds. Afterward, they celebrate with food and dancing, happy to relax after their hard work and to enjoy life.

Timeline

CHILEAN HISTORY

Settlers reach Monte Verde. **ca. 12,600 BCE**

The Chinchorro settle in northern Chile.   **6000 BCE**

Incas from Peru invade Chile.   **ca. 1470 CE**

Portuguese explorer Ferdinand Magellan   **1520**
passes through the strait off Chile
that now bears his name.

Diego de Almagro leads the first   **1535**
Spanish expedition into Chile.

Pedro de Valdivia founds Santiago.   **1541**

A Mapuche named Caupolicán helps   **1553**
lead a rebellion against the Spanish.

Ambrosio O'Higgins becomes   **1788**
governor of Chile.

WORLD HISTORY

ca. 2500 BCE   The Egyptians build the pyramids
and the Sphinx in Giza.

ca. 563 BCE   The Buddha is born in India.

313 CE   The Roman emperor Constantine
legalizes Christianity.

610   The Prophet Muhammad begins
preaching a new religion called Islam.

1054   The Eastern (Orthodox) and Western
(Roman Catholic) Churches break apart.

1095   The Crusades begin.

1215   King John seals the Magna Carta.

1300s   The Renaissance begins in Italy.

1347   The plague sweeps through Europe.

1453   Ottoman Turks capture Constantinople,
conquering the Byzantine Empire.

1492   Columbus arrives in North America.

1500s   Reformers break away from the Catholic
Church, and Protestantism is born.

1776   The U.S. Declaration of Independence
is signed.

1789   The French Revolution begins.

CHILEAN HISTORY

Chile declares independence from Spain. **1810**

Bernardo O'Higgins leads Chileans and **1817** Argentines to victory against Spanish forces, assuring the country's independence.

The first railway system in South **1851** America is completed in Chile.

Chilean forces defeat the Mapuche. **1881**

Chile wins the War of the Pacific and **1884** gains new land from Peru and Bolivia.

Government forces kill hundreds **1907** of striking miners in Iquique.

The largest recorded earthquake ever **1960** hits the area around Valdivia.

Salvador Allende is elected the first **1970** socialist president in Latin America.

Military leaders force Allende from power **1973** and begin a harsh crackdown; General Augusto Pinochet emerges as the new leader.

Pinochet loses a vote that would let him **1988** serve as president for another eight years.

Chile has its first free political **1989** election since 1973.

Michelle Bachelet becomes **2006** Chile's first female president.

Students protest in Santiago, **2011–2012** demanding free education.

WORLD HISTORY

1865 The American Civil War ends.

1879 The first practical lightbulb is invented.

1914 World War I begins.

1917 The Bolshevik Revolution brings communism to Russia.

1929 A worldwide economic depression begins.

1939 World War II begins.

1945 World War II ends.

1969 Humans land on the Moon.

1975 The Vietnam War ends.

1989 The Berlin Wall is torn down as communism crumbles in Eastern Europe.

1991 The Soviet Union breaks into separate states.

2001 Terrorists attack the World Trade Center in New York City and the Pentagon near Washington, D.C.

2004 A tsunami in the Indian Ocean destroys coastlines in Africa, India, and Southeast Asia.

2008 The United States elects its first African American president.

Timeline **129**

Fast Facts

Official name:	Republic of Chile
Capital:	Santiago
Official language:	Spanish
Official religion:	None

Santiago

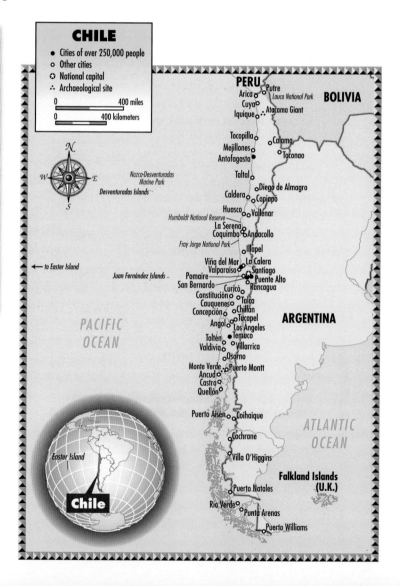

CHILE

- ● Cities of over 250,000 people
- ○ Other cities
- ⬡ National capital
- ∴ Archaeological site

0   400 miles
0   400 kilometers

PERU

BOLIVIA

Arica
Cuya
Iquique
Putre
Lauca National Park
Atacama Giant

Tocopilla
Mejillones
Antofagasta
Calama
Toconao

Taltal

Nazca-Desventuradas
Marine Park

Desventuradas Islands

Caldera
Diego de Almagro
Copiapó

Huasco
Vallenar

Humboldt National Reserve

La Serena
Coquimbo
Andacollo

Fray Jorge National Park

Illapel

to Easter Island

Juan Fernández Islands

Viña del Mar
Valparaíso
Pomaire
San Bernardo
La Calera
Santiago
Puente Alto
Rancagua
Curicó
Talca
Constitución
Cauquenes
Concepción
Chillán
Angol
Tucapel
Los Angeles
Toltén
Valdivia
Temuco
Villarrica
Osorno

PACIFIC
OCEAN

ARGENTINA

Monte Verde
Ancud
Castro
Quellón
Puerto Montt

Puerto Aisén
Coihaique

ATLANTIC
OCEAN

Cochrane

Villa O'Higgins

Falkland Islands
(U.K.)

Puerto Natales

Río Verde
Punta Arenas
Puerto Williams

Easter Island

Chile

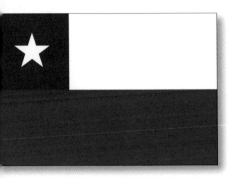

National flag

Skiing in the Andes

Founding date:	September 18, 1810, independence from Spain declared; February 12, 1818, official declaration of independence
National anthem:	"Himno Nacional de Chile" ("National Anthem of Chile")
Type of government:	Republic
Head of state:	President
Head of government:	President
Bordering countries:	Peru to the north, Bolivia to the northeast, and Argentina to the east
Area:	291,930 square miles (756,100 sq km)
Length of country north–south:	2,654 miles (4,270 km)
Width of country east–west:	Average of 110 miles (177 km)
Highest elevation:	Ojos del Salado, 22,572 feet (6,880 m)
Lowest elevation:	Sea level along the coast
Longest river:	Loa, 275 miles (440 km)
Average high temperature:	In Santiago, 85°F (29°C) in January; 58°F (14°C) in July
Average low temperature:	In Santiago, 53°F (12°C) in January; 37°F (3°C) in July
Highest average annual precipitation:	About 200 inches (500 cm), at the Strait of Magellan
Lowest average annual precipitation:	Arica, 0.03 inches (0.08 cm)

Moai statues

Currency

National population (2015 est.): 17,508,260

Population of major cities (2014 est.):

Santiago	5,128,041
Puente Alto	802,109
Antofagasta	390,832
San Bernardo	316,094
Viña del Mar	288,329
Temuco	264,642

Landmarks:
- ▶ *Funiculars*, Valparaíso
- ▶ *La Moneda*, Santiago
- ▶ *Lauca National Park*, Putre
- ▶ *Moai statues*, Easter Island
- ▶ *Wooden Churches*, Chiloé

Economy: Chile has a strong economy. It is the world's leading producer of copper. It also mines iron ore, gold, and other important minerals. Chile grows more grapes than any other country in South America. Other important agricultural products include apples, pears, avocados, cherries, nuts, and sugar beets. Forestry and fishing are key sectors of the export economy. Many manufacturing industries include oil refining and the production of textiles, plastics, and iron. About 62 percent of Chileans work in the service sector of the economy. This includes the selling of goods in stores, banking, insurance, education, health care, and government work.

Currency: Chilean peso. In 2016, US$1.00 equaled 727 Chilean pesos.

System of weights and measures: Metric system

Literacy rate (2015): 97.5%

Schoolchildren

Alexis Sánchez

Common Spanish words and phrases:

sí	yes
no	no
por favor	please
gracias	thank you
de nada	you're welcome
buenos días	good morning
adiós	good-bye
¿Cómo está usted?	How are you?
muy bien	very well
¿Dónde está…?	Where is…?

Prominent Chileans:

Isabel Allende   (1942–)
Author

Salvador Allende   (1908–1973)
Politician

Caupolicán   (?–1558)
Mapuche leader

Gabriela Mistral   (1889–1957)
Nobel Prize–winning poet

Pablo Neruda   (1904–1973)
Nobel Prize–winning poet

Violeta Parra   (1917–1967)
Singer and artist

Augusto Pinochet   (1915–2006)
General and leader of the military government

Alexis Sánchez   (1988–)
Soccer player

To Find Out More

Books

▶ Agosín, Marjorie. *I Lived on Butterfly Hill*. Translated by E. M. O'Connor. New York: Atheneum Books for Young Readers, 2014.

▶ Nagle, Jeanne, and Mary Main. *Isabel Allende: Award-Winning Author*. New York: Enslow Publishing, 2016.

▶ Peppas, Lynn. *The Atacama Desert*. New York: Crabtree Publishing, 2013.

▶ Reef, Catherine. *Poetry Came in Search of Me: The Story of Pablo Neruda*. Greensboro, NC: Morgan Reynolds, 2012.

▶ Scott, Elaine. *Buried Alive!* New York: Houghton Mifflin Harcourt, 2012.

Video

▶ *Pablo Neruda: The Life Story of Chile's Greatest Poet*. Kultur International Films, 2013.

▶ *Passport to Adventure: Patagonia North & South Aysen*. TravelVideoStore.com, 2012.

▶ Visit this Scholastic Web site for more information on Chile:
www.factsfornow.scholastic.com
Enter the keyword Chile

Index

Page numbers in *italics*
indicate illustrations.

A

Afro-Chilean people, 89, *89*
agriculture
    crops, 11, *20*, 40, *70*, 72–73, 75
    early people, 40
    economy and, 46, 75
    employment in, *70*, 72
    encomienda system, 43, 44, 47
    exports, 73
    food processing, 73–74
    government and, 54–55
    grapes, *70*, 73, 75
    Inca people, 41
    livestock, 18, 54, 108, 116, *116*
    manufacturing and, 76
    Mapuche people, 40
    nuts, 74, *74*
    Sur region, 54
    tree farming, 21
    Valle Central, 20, *20*
    walnuts, 74
Alessandri, Arturo, 53
Alexis (soccer player), 123, *123*
Alianza (Alliance) Party, 63
Allende, Isabel, 43, 104, *104*, 133
Allende, Salvador, 54, 55, *55*, 56, 57,
    65, 103, 133
Almagro, Diego de, 41–42, *44*
alpacas, 28, 30, *30*

altiplano (high plain) region, 17,
    29–30
amphibian life, *32*, 33
Andacollo, 93–94, *94*
Andean Carnival, *112*
Andes Mountains, 8, 9, 13, *24*, 30, 124
Anglican Church, 94–95
animal life
    alpacas, 28, 30, *30*
    altiplano region, 29–30
    birds, *26*, 27, 30, *30*, 31, 32, 33,
        35–36, 37
    burrowing parrots, 33
    Chiloé Island, 37
    chinchillas, 29
    coastal regions, 28, 36
    coipos, 31
    colocolos, 29–30
    cormorants, 36
    degus, 32–33
    Easter Islands, 37
    Fray Jorge National Park, 31
    giant otters, 35
    guanacos, 36, *36*
    Hudsonian godwits, 37
    hummingbirds, 27, 33, 37
    islands, 37
    Juan Fernández firecrowns, 37
    kodkods, 32
    Lauca National Park, 30, *30*
    livestock, 18, 54, 108, 116, *116*
    llamas, 28
    Magellanic penguins, *26*, 36
    Magellanic woodpeckers, 35–36
    mountains, 29–30
    Norte Chico region, 31
    Patagonia region, *26*, 36
    Peruvian song sparrows, 27
    pumas, 29, *29*
    rheas, 30, *30*
    rodeos, 123, *125*, 126
    sea otters, 31, *31*

    southern pudus, 35
    tarucas, 29
    temperate rain forests, 34–35
    Tierra del Fuego, 36
    Torres del Paine National Park, *30*
    Valle Central, 32–33
    vicuñas, 28
    viscachas, 29
    wildcats, 29–30, *29*, 32
    Zona Austral, 36
Antarctica, 15, 37, 75
Antofagasta, *17*, 19, *19*, 72
Arab immigrants, 84–85
architecture, 8, 67, 68, 85, 99
Armed Forces Day, 125, 126
art, 109–110, *110*
Astro (musical group), 107
Atacama Desert, 9, *11*, 15, 23, *23*, 27,
    28, *28*, 40, 51
Atacama Giant geoglyph, 40
Atlantic Ocean, 14, 22
Aymara people, 28, 87, 91

B

Bachelet, Michelle, 58, *60*, 61, 65, 73,
    85, 86
Baha'i religion, 96
Baker River, 22, 77
banking industry, 78
Barros Luco, Ramón, 121
Barros Luco (sandwich), 121, *121*
Basque language, 82
Basque people, 82
bellflower. *See* copihue (national
    flower).
beverages, 119–120, *119*
bicycles, 118, *118*, 124, 126
birds, *26*, 27, 30, *30*, 31, 32, 33, 35–36,
    37
Bolaño, Roberto, 104, *104*
Bolivia, 50–51, 53
Bonaparte, Napoleon, 47

borders, 13, 51
bottlenose dolphins, 31–32
Buddhism, 96
burrowing parrots, 33

C

Cape Horn, 22
capital city. *See* Santiago.
Carerra Pinto, Ignacio, 79, *79*
Carnicer, Ramón, 64
Carrera, Javiera, 47
Carrera, José Miguel, 47, 79
castellano language, 82
Caupolicán (Mapuche leader), 44, *44*, 133
Chamber of Deputies, 61–62, 63
Charles IV, king of Spain, 47
Charles V, king of Spain, 43, 91
chemical industry, 77
chess, *80*
children, 86, 93, *93*, 116, *117*, 124, *126*
Chilean peso (currency), 79, *79*
Chilean Supreme Court Building, 68
Chilean Trail, 124
Chilenismos (expressions), 84
Chiloé Island, 14, 21, 37, 99, *99*, 120
chinchillas, 29
Chinchorro people, 39, 40, *40*
Chinese immigrants, 84
Choapa River, 18
Chono people, 99
Christian Democratic Party, 54, 58, 63
Christmas holiday, 127
Cienfuegos, Gonzalo, 110
cities. *See also* Santiago; Valparaíso; towns; villages.
    Antofagasta, *17*, 19, *19*, 72
    Coquimbo, 25, 96
    Iquique, 52
    Puente Alto, 19
    Puerto Varas, 85
    San Bernardo, 19

Temuco, 19, 84
    Valdivia, 14, *14*, 43, 52, 84
civil war, 49, 82
climate, 9, 16, 18, 22–25, *25*, 28, 40
climate change, 40
clothing, 108, *117*
coat of arms. *See* national coat of arms.
coihue tree, 36
coipos, 31
colocolos, 29–30
communications, 49, 56
communism, 54
comptroller general, 65–66
Concepción, 43, 52
Congress. *See* National Congress.
conquistadoras, 43
conquistadores, 43
constitution, 49, 53, 61, 66, 91
Constitutional Court, 68
copihue (national flower), 31, *31*
copper mining, 15, 49, *51*, 53, 54, 58–59, 71–72, *72*, 75
Coquimbo, 25, 96
cormorants, 36
courts of appeal, 68
crafts, *100*, 101, 110–111, *111*
Cuasimodo festival, *126*, 127
currency (Chilean peso), 79, *79*

D

dance, 101, 107, 108–109, *108*, *112*, 126
Darwin's frogs, *32*
degus, 32–33
Diaguita people, 40
"disappeared," 56
diseases, 88
divorce, 92
Donoso, José, 103–104
Drake, Sir Francis, 46
drinking water, 25, *25*, 115
Duclos, Arturo, 109

E

early people, 39–40
earthquakes, 13–14, *14*
Easter holiday, 127
Easter Island, 14–15, 33, 37, 87, 88, 88, 90, 109, *109*
economy
    agriculture, 46, 75
    banking industry, 78
    comptroller general, 65–66
    currency (Chilean peso), 79, *79*
    employment, 11, 52–53, 54, 56, 70, 72, 78, 79, 83, 116
    exports, 11, 71, 73, 74, *74*
    fishing industry, 75–76, 76
    foreign investments, 49, 78
    forestry industry, 74–75, *74*, 77
    government and, 78
    Great Britain and, 49
    Great Depression, 53
    immigration and, 83
    imports, 71
    manufacturing, 52, 75, 76–77, 77
    military coups and, 56
    mining, 11, 15, 19, 47, 49, *51*, 52–53, 54, 58–59, 71–72, *72*, 73, 75
    service industries, 77–79
    strength of, 71
    taxes, 46, 48, 51
    technology industry, 78, 78
    tourism, 9, 11, *12*, 21, 78–79, 79
    United States and, 49, 53–54
    wealth gap, 115
education, 49, 63, 78, 116–117
elections, 47, 49, 50, 53, 54, 57, 58, 63, 65, 69, 69
electricity, 77
Elqui River, 18
El Tatio geyser field, 18, *18*
emigration, 86

employment, 11, 52–53, 54, 56, *70*, 72, 78, 79, 83, 116

encomienda system, 43, *43*, 44, 47

Ercilla, Alonso de, 102

European colonization, 20–21, 42–43, *42*, 43–44, *44*, 44–45, 81, 87–88, 91, 105, 106

European exploration, 15, *15*, 41–42, *44*

European Extremely Large Telescope, 78

executive branch, 46–47, 47–48, *48*, 49, 53, 54, 55, *55*, 56, 58, *58*, 60, 61, 62, 63, 65–66, *65*, 66, 68, 73, 86, 121

exports, 11, 71, 73, 74, *74*

F

families, 86, *114*, 119

Fernández y Solar, Juana, 93

Fernando, king of Spain, 47

film industry, 111

fishing industry, 75–76, *76*

fjords, 21–22

folk music, 106, *106*, 107

food processing, 52, 73, *77*

foods, 85, 119, 120, *120*, 121, *121*, 125–126

forestry industry, 74–75, *74*, 76

forests, 20, 21, 31, 34, 35, *35*, 74

Fray Jorge National Park, 31

G

games, *80*, 124, *124*

General Carrera Lake, 16, 22, *22*

geoglyphs, 40

geography
    altiplano region, 17
    borders, 13, 51
    coastline, *14*, 16, 17, *17*, 53
    deserts, 9, *11*, 15, 23, *23*
    earthquakes, 13–14, *14*
    elevation, 16, 17
    fjords, 21–22
    geysers, 18, *18*
    glaciers, 22
    islands, 14–15, 21
    lakes, 16, 21, 22, *22*
    land area, 13, 16
    mountains, 8, 9, 13, 17, *24*
    Norte Chico region, 18
    Norte Grande region, 15, 17
    rivers, 16, 17, 18, 22, 77
    Strait of Magellan, 14, 15
    Sur region, 20–21
    tectonic plates, 13–14
    Valle Central region, 18, 20
    volcanoes, 13, 18
    Zona Austral region, 21–22, *21*

German immigrants, 84, 85, 95

geysers, 18, *18*

Giant Magellan Telescope, 78, *78*

giant otters, 35

glaciers, 22

González, Tomás, 124

government
    Alianza (Alliance) Party, 63
    Chamber of Deputies, 61–62, 63
    Christian Democrats, 54, 58, 63
    coalitions, 62–63
    communism, 54
    comptroller general, 65–66
    conservation and, 21, 34, 77
    conservatives, 48, 49, 53, 54, 63
    constitution, 49, 53, 61, 66, 91
    Constitutional Court, 68
    courts of appeal, 68
    divorce and, 92
    economy and, 78
    education and, 49, 63, 116
    elections, 47, 49, 50, 53, 54, 57, 58, 63, 65, 69, 69
    electricity and, 77
    employment and, 54, 78
    executive branch, 46–47, 47–48, 48, 49, 53, 54, 55, 55, 56, 57, 58, 58, 60, 61, 62, 63, 65–66, 65, 66, 68, 73, 86, 121
    immigration and, 84
    independence, 47–48, 61, 79, 92
    judicial branch, 62, 63, 68, 68
    legislative branch, 49, 53, 57, 60, 61–62, 68
    liberals, 50, 54
    lithium mining and, 73
    Mapuche people and, 51–52, 59, *59*
    military, 15, 51
    military coup, 11, 55–56, *56*, 58, 103
    military courts, 68
    mining and, 54
    municipal governments, 69
    National Congress, 49, 53, 57, 60, 61–62, 63, 65, 68
    political parties, 54, 58, 62–63
    presidents, 49, 53, 54, 55, 56, 57, 58, *58*, 60, 61, 62, 63, 65–66, *65*, 66, 68, 69, 73, 85, *85*, 86, 121
    provincial governments, 69
    radicals, 50, 54
    regional governments, 69
    religion and, 91, 96
    runoff elections, 65
    Senate, 57, 61, 62, 63, 65, 68
    socialists, 54, 58, 63
    Spain and, *42*, 43, 46
    Supreme Court, 68, 68
    women in, 58, 65, *65*

Gran Torre Santiago, 67, *67*

grapes, *70*, 73, 75

Great Britain, 10, 19, 49, 84

Great Depression, 53

Great North region. *See* Norte Grande region.

greetings, 119

guanacos, 36, *36*
gymnastics, 124

H

health care, 58, 98
"Himno Nacional de Chile" (national anthem), 64
historical maps. *See also* maps.
    European Exploration and Settlement, *44*
    Indigenous Groups (1400), *41*
    War of the Pacific, *52*
holidays
    national, *108*, 113, 125–126, 127
    religious, 127
housing, *19*, 58, 115, 116
Hudsonian godwits, 37
huemul (national animal), 37
Huidobro, Vicente, 103
Humboldt National Reserve, 31
hummingbirds, 27, 33, 37
hydroelectricity, 77

I

immigration, 10–11, 46–47, 49, 54, 82–83, *83*, 84–85, 91, 95, 96. *See also* people.
imports, 71
Inca people, 41, 81
independence, 48, 61, 79, 92, 96
Independence Day, 125–126
indigenous people. *See also* Mapuche people; people.
    Aymara, 28, 87, 91
    Chinchorro, 39, 40, *40*
    Chono, 99
    class system and, 46
    Diaguita, 40
    diseases and, 88
    encomienda system, 43, 44, 47
    map of, *41*
    Rapa Nui, 33, 87–88, *88*, 109

religion and, 91
    slavery, 88
International Song Festival, 19
Iquique, 52
Islamic religion, 84, 96, *96*

J

Jara, Victor, 57, *57*
Jehovah's Witnesses, 95
jewelry, *100*, 111
Jodorowsky, Alejandro, 111
Juan Fernández firecrowns, 37
Juan Fernández fur seal, 33
Juan Fernández Islands, 14, 37, *76*
Judaism, 96
judicial branch of government, 62, 63, 68, *68*
junta groups, 55, 103

K

kodkod (wildcat), 32

L

labor strikes, 52–53
La Calera, 85
Lake District, 21
La Moneda building, *56*, 66, 67
languages, 10, 64, 82, 87, 113
La Portada arch, *17*
La Roja (national soccer team), 123
Larraín, Pablo, 111
Lauca National Park, 30, *30*
Lautaro (Mapuche fighter), 44
legislative branch of government, 49, 53, 57, 60, 61–62, 68
lenga trees, 36
Lillo, Eusebio, 64
literature, 43, 102–104, *102*, *103*, *104*, 133
lithium mining, 73, *73*
Little North region. *See* Norte Chico region.

livestock, 18, 54, 108, 116, *116*
llamas, 28
Llanquihue Lake, 21
Loa River, 16, 17
lomas, 27
Los Tres (musical group), 107

M

machi (shaman), 97–98, *97*, 101
Magellan, Ferdinand, 15, *15*, 36, 41, *44*
Magellanic lizards, 37
Magellanic penguins, 26, 36
Magellanic woodpeckers, 35–36
Maipú, *126*
manufacturing, 52, 75, 76–77, *77*, 78, *78*
maps. *See also* historical maps.
    political, *10*
    population density, 82
    resources, *74*
    Santiago, *67*
    topographical, *16*
Mapuche people. *See also* indigenous people; people.
    agriculture, 40
    ancestors of, 81
    Caupolicán, 44, *44*, 133
    Chiloé Island, 99
    choiquepurun dance, 108
    crafts, *100*, 101
    dance, 101
    encomienda system and, 44
    families, 86
    government and, 51–52, 59, *59*
    health care, 98
    housing, 115
    Inca and, 41
    lands of, 10, 18, 19, 52, 59, 86
    language and, 82, 87
    literature and, 102
    machi (shaman), 97–98, *97*, 101
    music, 101

palin (game), 124
population, 86
religion of, 91, 93, 97–98, 97, 101
Roman Catholicism and, 93
in Santiago, 44, 59
Spanish settlers and, 43, 44, 45, 45, 46, 49
Sur region, 20
Temuco and, 19
Mapudungun language, 87
Marble Cathedral, 22
marine life, 31, 32, 33, 37, 75–76, 76
marriage, 92
Matta, Roberto, 109
Mazika (musical group), 107
Mediterranean climate, 25
Mena, Javiera, 107
mestizo people, 45, 81
Methodist Church, 95
Methodist Pentecostal Church, 95
Metropolitan Cathedral, 67, 92
Metro system, 118
military, 15, 51
military coup, 11, 55–56, 56, 58, 103
military courts, 68
mining, 11, 15, 19, 41, 43, 47, 49, 51, 52–53, 54, 58–59, 71–72, 72, 73, 73, 75
Mistral, Gabriela, 102, 103, 133
molybdenum mining, 72
monkey puzzle tree (national monument), 34, 34
Monte Verde settlement, 39
Montt, Manuel, 49
Mormonism, 95
mosques, 96, 96
moss, 35
mummies, 39, 40, 40
municipal governments, 69
murals, 110, 110
music, 19, 57, 64, 101, 105–107, 105, 106, 107

My Invented Country (Isabel Allende), 104

N
names, 84, 85
national anthem, 64
national coat of arms, 37
National Congress, 49, 53, 57, 60, 61–62, 63, 65, 68
national dance, 108–109, 108
national drink, 120
national flag, 64, 66, 66
national flower, 31, 31
National History Museum, 67
national holidays, 108, 113, 125–126, 127
national monument, 34
national parks, 12, 21, 30, 30, 79
national soccer team, 123
national sports, 123
Nazca-Desventuradas Marine Park, 33
Neruda, Pablo, 103, 103, 111, 133
New Year's Day, 126
nitrate mining, 52–53
Nobel Prize, 102, 103
Norte Chico (Little North) region, 18, 24, 25, 31
Norte Grande (Great North) region, 15, 17, 23–24, 30
nuts, 74, 74

O
Obama, Barack, 104
observatories, 17, 78, 78
O'Higgins, Ambrosio, 46–47
O'Higgins, Bernardo, 47, 48, 48
oil industry, 77
Ojos del Salado Lake, 16
Ojos del Salado volcano, 18
Olympic Games, 124

P
Pacific Ocean, 9, 14, 17, 22, 124
Parra, Angel, 107
Parra, Violeta, 107, 133
Pascua River, 77
Patagonia region, 9–10, 21, 21, 25, 26, 36, 77, 79, 117, 119, 122
Pedro Montt, 112
pejerrey chilenos, 33
Pentecostals, 95
people. *See also* immigration; indigenous people; Mapuche people.
Afro-Chileans, 89, 89
Basques, 82
bedtime, 119
children, 86, 93, 93, 116, 117, 124, 126
clothing, 108, 117
"disappeared," 56
diseases, 88
divorce, 92
early people, 39–40
education, 49, 63, 78, 116–117
emigration, 86
employment, 11, 52–53, 54, 56, 70, 72, 78, 79, 83, 116
families, 86, 114, 119
foods, 85, 119, 120, 120, 121, 121, 125–126
games, 80, 124, 124
greetings, 119
health care, 58, 98
housing, 19, 58, 115, 115
Inca, 41, 81
languages, 10, 64, 82, 87, 113
leisure time, 119, 119
marriage, 92
mestizos, 45, 81
middle class, 114, 116
moving, 116
mummies, 39, 40, 40

names, 84, 85
population, 9, 19, *46*, 67, *82*, 84
poverty, 56, 58, 115
refugees, 85
slavery, 41, 43, 45–46, 47, 81, 88
social classes, 45–46, 52
Spanish, 82–83
urban areas, 114–115
voting rights, 69
wealth gap, 115
weddings, 126
women, 54, 58, 65, 85, 89, 98, *102*, *112*
Peru, 50–51
Peru Current, 75
Peruvian song sparrows, 27
Pinochet, Augusto, 11, 55, 56, 57, *58*, 65, 93, 103, 107, 111, 133
plant life
    Atacama Desert, 27, 28
    coastal regions, 36
    coihue tree, 36
    forests, 20, 21, 31, 34, 35, *35*, 74
    islands, 37
    lenga trees, 36
    lomas, 27
    monkey puzzle trees, 34, *34*
    moss, *35*
    mountains, 30
    murtas, 36
    Norte Grande region, 17
    quinoa, 30
    temperate rain forests, *35*
    trees, 20–21
    Valle Central, 34, *34*
Plaza de Armas, 67, *92*
poetry, 102–103, *103*, 133
political parties, 54, 58, 62–63
Pomaire, 111, *111*
Pontifical Catholic University of Chile, 117
population, 9, 19, 46, 67, 82, 84

Portales, Diego, 49
port cities, 19, *19*
Portillo ski resort, *24*
pottery making, 111, *111*
poverty, 56, 58, 115
Presbyterian Church, 95
presidents, 49, 53, 54, 55, 56, 57, 58, *58*, 60, 61, 63, 65, *65*, 66, *66*, 68, 69, 73, 85, *85*, 86, 121
Protestantism, 94–95, *95*
provincial governments, 69
Puente Alto, 19
Puerto Montt, 84
Puerto Varas, 85
pumas, 29, *29*

Q

queñoa tree, 30

R

railroads, 49, 53
Rapa Nui people, 33, 87–88, *88*, 109
recipe, 121, *121*
refugees, 85
regional governments, 69
Regional Museum of Araucanía, 19
religion. *See also* Roman Catholicism.
    Anglican Church, 94–95
    Baha'i, 96
    Buddhism, 96
    Chiloé Island, 99
    government and, 91, 96
    holidays, 127
    immigration and, 84–85, 91, 95, 96
    independence and, 96
    Islam, 84, 96, *96*
    Jehovah's Witnesses, 95
    Judaism, 96
    Mapuche people, 91, 93, 97–98, *97*, 101
    Methodist Church, 95
    Mormonism, 95

mosques, 96, *96*
music and, 101
Pentecostals, 95
Presbyterian Church, 95
Protestantism, 94–95, *95*
reptilian life, 37
rheas, 30, *30*
roadways, 53, 118
rodeo (national sport), 123, *125*, 126
Roman Catholicism. *See also* religion.
    Augusto Pinochet and, 93
    baptisms, 93, *93*
    Christmas holiday, 127
    conservatives and, 48
    conversos and, 96
    Cuasimodo festival, *126*
    Easter holiday, 127
    encomienda system and, 43
    holidays, 127
    independence and, 92
    indigenous people and, 91
    Mapuche people and, 93
    mass, 90
    Metropolitan Cathedral, 67, *92*
    rites, 93
    saints, 93, *93*
    Santiago, 92, *92*
    size of, 10, 91
    Spanish colonization and, 91
    Teresa of the Andes (saint), 93, *93*
    Virgin Mary, 94, *94*
runoff elections, 65

S

saints, 93, *93*
San Bernardo, 19
Sánchez, Alexis, 123, *123*, 133, *133*
sandwiches, 120, 121, *121*
San Martín, José de, 47
Santiago. *See also* cities.
    architecture in, 8, 67, *67*

Chilean Supreme Court Building, 68

climate, 16

foreign investment in, 78

founding of, 67

government in, 61

independence and, 46

La Moneda building, 56, 66, 67

manufacturing in, 52

map of, 67

Mapuche people in, 44, 59

Metropolitan Cathedral, 67, 92

mosques in, 96

music in, 105

New Year's Day in, 126

Plaza de Armas, 67, 92

Pontifical Catholic University of Chile, 117

population of, 9, 19, 46, 67, 80, 84

Protestantism in, 95

Roman Catholicism in, 92, 92

University of Chile, 117

seafood, 120

sea otters, 31, 31

Senate, 57, 61, 62, 63, 65, 68

Sendero de Chile (Chilean Trail), 124

service industries, 77–79

shipping industry, 19, 49

silver mining, 49, 51

skiing, 124, 124

slavery, 41, 43, 45–46, 47, 81, 88

snowboarding, 124

soccer, 123, 123, 133, 133

southern pudus, 35

Spanish colonization, 42–43, 42, 43–44, 44–45, 46, 81, 91, 105, 106

Spanish exploration, 15, 15, 41–42

Spanish language, 10, 64, 82, 113

Spanish settlers, 82–83

sports, 24, 123–124, 123, 125, 133, 133

Strait of Magellan, 14, 15, 16, 41

Suarez, Inés de, 43

subway, 118

summer sports, 124

Supreme Court, 68, 68

Sur (South) region, 20–21, 54

T

tarucas, 29

taxes, 46, 48, 51

tea, 116, 119, 119

technology industry, 78, 78

tectonic plates, 13–14

telescopes, 78, 78

temperate rain forests, 35–36, 35

Temuco, 19, 84

tennis, 123

Teresa of the Andes (saint), 93, 93

Tierra del Fuego, 14, 15, 22, 36, 41

Tijoux, Ana, 107, 107

Torres del Paine National Park, 12, 30

tourism, 9, 11, 12, 21, 78–79, 79

towns. See also cities; villages.
  Andacollo, 93–94, 94
  La Calera, 85
  Pomaire, 111, 111
  Puerto Montt, 84, 112

transportation, 9, 19, 49, 53, 118

tree farming, 21

Tucapel fort, 44

U

unions, 52, 56

United States, 49, 53–54, 55, 104

University of Chile, 117

V

Valdivia, 14, 14, 43, 52, 84

Valdivia, Pedro de, 42–43, 42, 44, 44

Valle Central (Central Valley) region, 18, 20, 25, 32–33, 34, 85

Vallejo, Camila, 63, 63

Valley of the Moon, 11

Valparaíso. See also cities.
  architecture, 19
  funiculars in, 19

growth of, 50

murals, 110, 110

National Congress in, 60, 61

New Year's Day in, 126

population of, 114

shipping industry in, 49

"Venceremos" (Victor Jara), 57

vicuñas, 28

villages. See also cities; towns.
  early people, 39, 40
  drinking water, 25
  fishing industry, 75

Viña del Mar (Vineyard of the Sea), 19, 84

Virgin Mary, 94, 94

viscachas, 29

volcanoes, 13

voting rights, 69

W

walnuts, 74

War of the Pacific, 51, 52, 53, 79, 89

water, 25, 115

water sports, 124

weddings, 126

wildcats, 29–30, 29, 32

wildflowers, 28, 28

wildlife. See amphibian life; animal life; marine life; plant life; reptilian life.

wine, 119–120

winter sports, 124

women, 54, 58, 65, 85, 89, 98, 102, 112

Wood, Andrés, 111

World War I, 53

World War II, 53

Z

Zamorano, Iván "Bam Bam," 123

Zona Austral (Southern Zone) region, 21–22, 21, 36, 37

Meet the Author

MICHAEL BURGAN HAS BEEN WRITING BOOKS for children for more than twenty years, producing more than 250 titles. For the Enchantment of the World series, he has written about Belgium, the United States, Kenya, and Malaysia. Burgan has a BA in history from the University of Connecticut. He currently lives in Santa Fe, New Mexico. In his spare time, he enjoys writing plays, traveling, cooking, and photography.

This is the second time Burgan has written about Chile, and he used a variety of sources to learn about the country's history and geography. He started with travel guides and scholarly books. The histories ranged from general views of Chile's past to books on specific topics, such as the 1973 takeover by General Pinochet.

He then turned to Web sites, especially ones from the U.S. government, international organizations, and the Chilean government. One key source for current events was the online version of the *Santiago Times* and a related paper, the *Patagonia Regional Times*. Burgan also was lucky enough to have a friend who put him in contact with Miguel Leiva Reyes, a Chilean who gave him insight into daily life in Chile.

Photo Credits

Photographs ©:

Maps by Mapping Specialists.